SON OF THE VIKINGS

Son of the Vikings

Josephine Cunnington Edwards

TEACH Services, Inc.
PUBLISHING
www.TEACHServices.com • (800) 367-1844

Facsimile Reproduction

As this book played a formative role in the development of Christian thought and the publisher feels that this book, with its candor and depth, still holds significance for the church today. Therefore the publisher has chosen to reproduce this historical classic from an original copy. Frequent variations in the quality of the print are unavoidable due to the condition of the original. Thus the print may look darker or lighter or appear to be missing detail, more in some places than in others.

ISBN-13: 978-1-4796-0816-4 (Paperback)
Library of Congress Control Number: 2017906494

Preface

This fascinating story, from the days when the Advent Movement was young, has its important lesson for a generation growing up in a society where persecution seems far past.

However, this may be just the time when such a story has a mission to warn many youth that problems of standing up for their faith and obeying God will in the future also demand a firm answer in spite of threat of loss of freedom or even life.

Oscar Engen, now an octogenarian still active in church and sanitarium work, has through his remarkable art of Christian living furnished his family and coming generations with a radiant example of faithfulness.

The people north of the Limfjord, the "Vendelbo" of Denmark, have through history shown themselves unusually fearless, sturdy, and dependable; and the hero of this book is no exception.

J. D. Henriksen, M.D., Health Secretary, Northern European Division of the General Conference of Seventh-day Adventists; former staff physician of Battle Creek Sanitarium, Michigan, and the Skodsborg Sanitarium, Denmark.

Preface

CHAPTER 1

On a farm up in North Jutland, the main peninsula of Denmark, about three miles from Frederikshavn, was born a lad, Oscar Engen. He descended from the fierce Vikings, who long ago pillaged England, Scotland, and Ireland. Situated on a lowland containing dunes and heaths, the farm huddled near the cold ocean; yet it prospered under the thrifty hand of Oscar's father. Dairy cattle munched the coarse grass springing from the sandy soil.

The old farm with its rambling, comfortable thatched-roof house, bore the name of Friedenstrand. It was a hive of activity, from the ruddy-faced dairymaids, who made butter and cheese, to the strong farmhands, who cared for the animals and tilled the reluctantly yielding soil.

A mother with gentle hands and a tender voice, who surrounded his small boyhood with the security of her love, filled Oscar's childhood memories of farm life. The servants adored her, though they knew she kept a sharp, though kindly, eye on their work. Beggars and wayfarers, braced against the wind, ragged sleeves shielding their chapped faces, sometimes came to the farm. Oscar's mother had a reputation for her kindness. They went away with full stomachs and her blessing.

Even in his later life Oscar could still in his mind see her sweeping crusts, crumbs, and peelings into her apron from the worktable of the long bright kitchen. Then she sped out to the pasture bars, where the horses came pounding across the pasture, manes flying, at the sight of her slight figure. Often the boy went with her. "Always be kind to animals, Oscar," she would say, her voice vibrant with the cadences of love.

"I will, Mother," the small lad promised.

"If you're kind to animals, you'll be kind to people," she told him. "We are gods to the animals. Oh, if we could only be as faithful to our wonderful God as Rover and Danke are to us! They never fail us."

"I will always remember, Mother."

He often thought of the day when he was a tiny boy clinging to his mother's hand until they led her out into the white-capped surf near Frederikshavn to a baptizing. Although Uncle Ottosen held his cold little hand, he could not help crying. He felt sure they were going to drown his mother.

Even before she went to the temporary shelter to change her soaked clothing, she clasped her fearful little child's head to her wet robe. "Darling, my precious one, I'm so happy!" she cried, to the little boy's wonderment. "I have gone down into the water of the ocean like Jesus went into the grave when He died for our sins. Now my sins are forgiven, and I can walk in a new life!"

"What sins, Mother?" he had cried out, for he could not remember ever seeing his mother do anything that he thought was wrong. "Why, Mother, you never made any sins!"

But she only smiled and waved her white hand at him reassuringly as she went to change her clothing.

Her brother, Dr. Carl Ottosen, had started the world-famed Skodsborg Sanitarium north of Copenhagen on the island of Sjælland (Zealand). Through him she learned of Christian education and of new methods of treating disease. But her own health was poor, so that even her skilled brother had to tell her that she did not have long to live.

In spite of her illness, a fierce Viking determination possessed her to put her children in church school some miles away. She made an agreement with Grandmother Ottosen to keep them five days a week, so that they could attend the school. Longing to build a firm religious foundation into their lives, she felt a fierce urgency, for she knew that her time was short. "I will need a horse, Chris," she quietly told her husband one day at the dinner table.

He stopped eating and looked at her. "A horse? For what?" he asked loudly.

"I will need a carriage, too, so that I can carry things to my mother. She will keep the children while they go to the church school there. I must take bread and cheese, blankets, and some extra pillows."

"A church school?" Oscar's father spit the phrase out as if it were an insect that had suddenly flown into his mouth. "What about the state school here?"

But her will was indomitable. "They must go to the church school, Chris," she said again. "And I must have a horse, a gentle driving horse."

In the end, her brusque husband took her to the horse market. They entered the big gates and saw animals the farmers from round about had brought to the market to sell. Although he did not want to buy the horse, Mr. Engen knew horses and determined no one should get the best of him. Suddenly, to his disgust, his wife, whom everyone *knew* could not tell a good animal from a poor one, called to him.

"Chris! Chris! Come here, Chris."

Hearing his wife's gentle voice in spite of the noise of the market, he stalked toward her slight figure, shaking his head in disgust at women's foibles. An old bay horse, with a drooping head, stood roped to a scraggly tree. She had bit sores in her mouth, and flies swarmed about the harness galls. One leg was swollen. The flesh was shiny, her skin so thin it seemed her body would burst out of it.

"I want *this* horse," Mrs. Engen said, laying her hand on the horse's tangled mane.

"You want what?" her husband shouted. "That's crowbait. It'll be dead tomorrow."

The owner said nothing but watched both of their faces intently.

"No, not if I get it home," she replied. "It has had ill-treatment, Chris. Someone will get her for almost nothing, and kill her getting his money's worth out of her. I'll put a heating compress on that swollen leg——"

"A heating *what?*" her husband asked incredulously.

"My brother, Dr. Ottosen, has learned about some wonderful treatments from America—a Dr. Kellogg, Chris. He uses them at the Skodsborg Sanitarium, and people get well. I'll have this horse well by the time school starts."

Mr. Engen looked at his wife for a moment, then he turned back to the owner. "I'll buy this miserable horse—for *her* sake, certainly not my own," he said shortly, with a look on his face not far from disdain. "I'll buy it if the price is right—and it had better be. Don't forget we've got some laws in Denmark, thank God, against cruelty to animals. I won't haggle with you. This animal has had some terrible cruelty. I wouldn't want to be a horse in *your* hands."

Its owner mentioned a price agreeable even to Chris. They fed and watered the creature before fastening her lead rope to the back of the buggy. Chris did not complain, nor did his wife have to ask him to drive slowly.

It was long past the supper hour when they got home. When his wife hurried to the barn with a bucket of water and an armful of cloths, Chris followed out of curiosity. In a little while she had the swollen leg wrapped thoroughly in dripping towels, then covered it with dry woolen cloths pinned securely.

"What's that supposed to do?" Chris asked, amused.

His wife straightened up and wiped the sweat from her high, blue-veined forehead. "You see, Chris," she explained, "the *blood* of the body is the *life*. The cold water on the horse's swollen leg will set up a reaction, so the blood of her body will rush down there to get the leg warm. We are *so* wonderfully made, Chris. I don't see how anyone could ever disbelieve in God!"

A little impatient, Chris turned away. If God, then, was so wonderful, why didn't he make his wife well? She was ailing, getting worse all the time. Dr. Ottosen himself had said that her disease was incurable. Was God just, taking such a good mother and leaving her little children alone?

The next morning Chris came into the barn as his wife put another "heating poultice" on the new horse's leg. He whistled. The swelling had almost vanished. His wife had washed the sores and galls on the horse's back with a solution of Epsom salts dissolved in water. Then she had applied a salve to keep gnats and flies from tormenting the creature. Afterward she led her out to the pasture to graze.

By the time school began, the sores had healed, and on Sunday afternoon the children and mother drove northward along the road by the sea to grandmother's and to church school. For several years the horse pulled Mrs. Engen and her children on their northward journey. Every Friday, Oscar's mother returned for them.

Then one Thursday evening she arrived unexpectedly to pick up the children.

The grandmother and an aunt, puzzled, went out to the buggy. "Why are you taking them home today, daughter?" the old woman asked. "Is there something wrong, something amiss at your house? It is not good for them to miss a day of school."

"I know that," mother answered in her patient voice, "but I shall not be able to come tomorrow. I knew I had to get them today."

The children ran out to meet their mother,

glad for the extra holiday. They gleefully climbed into the buggy for their homeward ride. Instead, it would be the saddest day of their lives.

The lamps did not go out all night in the long thatched farmhouse. Chris dispatched a hired man on horseback for the doctor. But it was no use. Mrs. Engen died that night.

The grandfather stood by her quaintly carved old bed. "I remember yesterday," he said, tears streaming down his wrinkled face. "She asked me to hitch up the horse. 'I hate to bother you,' she said, 'but maybe I won't have to ask you to do it again for me.' I'd have hitched that horse every day from now to doomsday for *her*. But she never wanted to be a bother and a trouble." Hard sobs racked his body.

The funeral and all of the other strange happenings distressed little Oscar. He tried to find out about the frightful riddle of death from anyone who would stop and listen to him. Grandmother told him that his mother had committed her children to the care of the Saviour. "And she prayed extra for you, Oscar."

"Mother did? Why, Grandma?"

"That I cannot tell you. I think she knew that because you often were a naughty boy, and had a bad temper, you might need special help from the angels."

"Do you think I do, Grandmother? I need

mother awful bad. I can't see why God took her away."

Grandmother pulled the little boy onto her lap, and patted and sang Danish lullabies to him while he sobbed out his puzzlement and grief.

CHAPTER 2

The journeys to the humble church school stopped abruptly after Mrs. Engen's burial in the churchyard.

Now began the routine of the state-operated school and of the duties their father assigned them. Their farm continued with the activity of making a living. Someone went regularly out to the ocean to fish. The family stored kegs of home-salted fish, and dried and wrapped large salmon to put away in boxes. The men butchered sheep, hogs, and cattle in the cold late fall. People hurried and scuttled everywhere, doing their never-ending round of chores. When spring finally came and the harsh North Sea winds became more balmy, they planted great gardens of potatoes, carrots, and lettuce.

Oscar peddled milk. He used a little horse cart to haul the milk cans, with a board laid across it to sit on, when he went into town. He was so regular in his schedule that he did not need the little bell he had to ring. The busy housewives bustled out with their pitchers and jugs, and Oscar measured out the milk to his regular customers.

One time the lad got tired of the monotonous drive to town with the hot sun beating down on his back. "I believe I'll crawl back there with the milk cans and take a nap," he told himself. "The horse knows the way to town as well as I do." Soon the boy fell asleep among the jostling cans.

Suddenly he sat up, alarmed. He could hear someone screaming, "The boy! The boy!" To Oscar's horror, the horse was leisurely crossing the railroad track, and the fast train, bound for Frederikshavn, hurtled toward them. He heard himself screaming, screaming, as the chuffing metal monster and certain death bore down upon him.

"Lord, help me!" he cried. Thoughts of his mother and grandmother and aunt, and the quiet old churchyard cemetery of grassy hummocks, where he would soon lie in a coffin made in the shape of the sole of a shoe, flashed through his mind.

On came the steam engine, shrieking, until its hot breath practically seared his face. He caught glimpses of women running from their houses, their eyes wide and their mouths open, screaming.

The horse and cart had barely cleared the track when the puffing engine rushed clanging past, the engineer and the fireman both yelling, the whistle splitting the air. The gatekeeper, too, was shouting, livid with fear. He had gotten too busy at something else to remember to close the gate. Then he had dozed off. He knew his mistake would cost him his reputation, his job, and maybe even his freedom.

After the train passed, an excited crowd surrounded the boy and cart. Oscar shook so much that he could not talk, but more thoughts raced through his mind than had in a year. "I'll never, never go to sleep again while I'm riding," he resolved fervidly. "I'll remember this day all my life. All my life I'll remember, and I won't forget what it is to be face to face with death."

CHAPTER 3

Influence is a powerful thing, especially on the mind of a little child. Children look up to adults and pattern their small lives on what they see in older people. One hired man had a particular impact on Oscar because he noticed the boy and took time to talk to him and answer his many questions.

The boy's face took on a certain glow when the hired man came around, for he felt bigger and more important because of the big Danish farmer's flattering attitude toward him. He became such a hero to the boy that if he had told Oscar in all sincerity that black was white or day was really night, the child would have almost believed him.

"Oscar," he said one day, "do you know why your name is Oscar?"

The child's face registered both puzzlement and surprise. "Why, no," he answered. "I think it is because my father and mother thought it was a good name."

"No," he said gravely. "No, you're wrong there. There was a bigger reason than that."

Little Oscar looked up quickly.

The farmer's dancing, merry eyes watched him. "You see, Oscar, long, long ago, all of the Scandinavian countries were united. Sweden, Norway, and Denmark were all one big country. It was the greatest country in *all* of Europe!"

Oscar's gaze never left the hired man's face as he bent over the child.

"Sh-sh-sh." The man's voice was low but resonant. "You were born to be *King Oscar* someday. You will unite the three kingdoms again, and be King Oscar, of Sweden, Norway, and Denmark."

To the child, Martin wasn't just a hired man forking hay and straw and manure, lowering the pasture bars, and caring for the livestock. He was a prophet, a seer, with occult powers to pierce into the future. Oscar believed him implicitly. Later, dreaming that he would someday live in a palace, all of his games centered about his great destiny.

One day strangers came into the yard where he played. "What is your name, little boy?" they asked.

He drew himself up to his full height. "I am not *just* a little boy," he asserted. "I am Oscar, the king of all Norway, Sweden, and Denmark."

The general laugh which greeted his reply angered him a little; but, even so, he thought, "When I get to be the king in the palace, I will show them all a thing or two."

Sometimes Oscar wondered about his mother's older brother, whom he called Uncle Ottosen, though he scarcely remembered him. Mrs. Engen had often spoken proudly of him as a wise man. He, too, kept the seventh-day Sabbath as Oscar's mother had done. She had often described to her children her brother's kindness to animals.

"Why, if one of the farm creatures got sick, my brother was right there and seemed to know just what to do. He saved the life of many a poor sick beast. 'You ought to be a veterinary doctor,' people always told him, and my brother Carl's eyes would gleam at that. It pleased him to think of helping poor suffering creatures. That's why he is such a good doctor today."

"Did Uncle Ottosen learn to be a—a——"

"A veterinary doctor?" their mother asked. She smiled. "He was taking the course to cure animals, and was almost finished," she said, her eyes glowing with pride. "Then the Lord came into our lives in a wonderful way and changed everything." Her voice was soft and vibrant.

"How, Mother, how?" the children eagerly inquired, crowding around her chair and watching her face. They had heard the story many times, but they loved to hear her tell it again.

"My brother Carl discovered more about the Bible," she told them, laying her thin hand on the worn covers of her copy. "He learned from an evangelist who came to Denmark to preach a new message. Oh, it was wonderful, for we had been Lutherans and thought we knew all that the Bible taught. But we didn't."

"Did he tell you and Uncle Ottosen all about what he learned, Mother?" someone always asked.

"Oh, yes!" she cried. "Evangelist Brodersen made it so plain that a child could understand. Then he talked to my brother and told him he ought to be a minister and go out and preach. 'You must go to Battle Creek, in America, Carl,' Evangelist Brodersen said. 'We have a fine college there, and you can go and learn to be a preacher.'

"My brother did just that! He wrote back to us about America and Battle Creek. There is a large hospital and a place called a sanitarium there, perhaps almost one of the biggest places like that in the world, he said. You know, one of Carl's friends, Johann Nordholm, is a nurse there. But, best of all, Carl met that important doctor at Battle Creek, Dr. John Harvey Kellogg. 'You *must* be a medical doctor,' he said to your uncle. 'God wants you to help people. They are more important than animals.' That settled Carl's mind. He had to work hard, but he came back to Denmark and took the medical course at the University of Copenhagen."

The children were proud of their Uncle Carl Ottosen, who operated a sanitarium in the suburbs north of Copenhagen on the island of Zealand. A friend of Dr. Kellogg's had spotted the two great houses at Skodsborg, part of the royal estate of the king, and saw their potential. In a beautiful location near the lapping waters of the sea, they formed the nucleus of what became at that time the largest Seventh-day Adventist sanitarium in the world.

Other medical men and institutions first scoffed at and then became alarmed at its hydrotherapy treatments. They loudly dubbed it the "Cabbage Hotel" because of its vegetarian principles. But patients poured into Skodsborg in such numbers that they had to build it larger. It became the most noted place of healing in all Europe. Royalty and important people from all over the world patronized it. Its influence grew, until in 1927 the Danish king knighted Dr. Ottosen.

CHAPTER 

Oscar, his brother, and his sisters continued to grow up on the busy farm after their mother's death. Of course, they had no more chance to go to church school, out on their wind-strafed acres of Jutland. Life had to go on, even though the ache of her loss continued. But the fragrance of her influence would never die.

The years passed, and the time approached when Oscar knew he must serve in the Danish army. The country had compulsory military training, and the young man wondered where he would like to serve. He thought of the King's Guard, of how they in splendid uniforms paraded before one of the four palaces at Amalienborg Square, the Danish king's winter residence. Then, with his father, he talked over the possibility of his entering the cavalry, for he was, he had learned to his sorrow, one-half inch too short to join the King's Guard.

He felt a certain amount of pride as he weighed such matters, for Oscar had a girl friend, a blonde girl whom he hoped one day to make his wife. Already he dreamed of a home which she presided over. To his mind she seemed ideal in every respect.

He wanted to impress her with his soldier's uniform. Then when his stint in the army ended, he could turn to farming or gardening for a living and—but his thoughts could not seem to go much further. He had a strange, indefinable feeling about his two years in the army—why, he could not tell. And he could not seem to lay any plans beyond that. In six months he must serve his country. Yet a strange dread filled his mind at the very thought of it. Oscar wondered what he should do with the time until his induction into the army.

Then unexpectedly there came a letter from Uncle Ottosen in Skodsborg. "Why don't you come here, Oscar, and work for me until you go into the army?" his uncle wrote. "It will give you some extra money. You will meet many new friends, and you can get acquainted with your aunt and me. Besides, you have never seen the sanitarium here. If it is good enough for royalty and the great of Europe, Oscar, you *must* see it!"

In the same week he had an offer to be assistant caretaker of a vast baronial estate. As he thought about the security he was striving for, it seemed far more sensible to take the work on the estate. If he did well there, he would be laying a foundation for his lifework. He could return after military service and settle down.

But somehow the letter from Uncle Ottosen attracted him more than he could understand. Against his better judgment, he favored his uncle's offer. Of course, his father opposed it, and so did his girl friend.

"So much waste and foolishness," his father admonished him. "That is not *your* work—peddling pills and dipping people into water. *My* sons are for the land and for the sea. You are not building your future at all. You must think of that! Are you insane?"

Oscar knew it didn't sound sensible. And when big slices of ham lay on the platter at mealtime, his father jibed him even further. "You won't get good food like *this,*" he said. "Do you want to become a weakling?" But in spite of his misgivings, he found himself on the train speeding on to Skodsborg to work for the six months before he entered military service.

CHAPTER

Before he left by train for the sanitarium, Oscar registered for the army. The law required all able-bodied young men to enter the Danish army sometime between the ages of eighteen and twenty-two. Since he had already passed his twenty-first birthday, he had to take the step as soon as possible.

A feeling of family pride swelled through Oscar during the train trip as he thought about how his uncle had started the "Badesanatorium," as people referred to it. His uncle had even his father's respect, for Ottosen had graduated from the University of Copenhagen.

Oscar knew from the old stories of his uncle and mother that part of the sanitarium's original physical plant was actually a palace, built for King Frederick VII. But because of Dr. John Harvey Kellogg's influence, the additional constructions and complex of buildings were painted a gleaming, glowing white, until to patients and visitors it became known as the "White Village." The landscaped buildings faced the Öre Sund, the sound which separates Denmark from Sweden at their closest point. Behind the "White Village" stretched the predominantly beech state forest.

Oscar quickly found his uncle, who greeted him warmly and took him to his comfortable home opposite the great institution's buildings.

His uncle told him of the progress the sanitarium had made and how it had become known all over Europe. "It's another Battle Creek, Oscar!" Ottosen exclaimed. "And we need to run it according to what God has revealed to us."

Oscar wondered what he meant but said nothing.

"From the beginning God has blessed us," his uncle continued. "We have not depended on drugs—and we have used hydrotherapy."

"What is that, Uncle?" Oscar asked.

"It is medical treatments, Oscar, by physical and natural means. Healing by baths, hot and cold applications of water to induce better circulation. It was Dr. Wilhelm Winternitz, of Austria, I believe, who actually put this type of healing onto a scientific basis. And I might say, it has succeeded beyond our fondest hopes."

"What else do you use besides water?" the young man inquired, interested in spite of himself. He could hardly believe such a simple thing could do much.

"We have the same kind of program they have at Battle Creek. We have medical exercises, massage, hot and cold baths, treatments with woolen cloth applications we call fomentations, and we put great stress on diet. We have had wonderful success. At the beginning we had room for only twenty patients. Now, you can see they are coming and going continually, and we have a long waiting list. Not just common people either; the elite and the nobility are coming our way."

Oscar had arrived at the sanitarium on a Friday. The place hummed with activity.

His uncle had told him that they would not show him the particular work he had to do until after the Sabbath. "Just go around and see the whole place," he had said. "Get acquainted with the layout. This will be your home for several months."

As Oscar walked around, he noticed particularly the cleanliness and the businesslike behavior of everyone. It suddenly came over him that everyone was "getting ready for Sabbath," just as his mother used to do. He could see the cooks hustling around in the kitchen, and when his nose told him that he was nearing the bakery, he saw that the bakers, too, aware of the sinking sun, were working hard so that they could be ready for the Sabbath. After supper, served in his uncle's pleasant dining room, Steen Rasmussen, his uncle's secretary, told Oscar that the church would hold a young people's meeting that night. Oscar was interested, for the young people he had already seen did not look like the fanatics some had assured him would be at the sanitarium. Instead, they seemed like normal young people seeking an honest livelihood, full of business and vigor. He went up to his room, dressed in his good clothes, and combed his fine mop of dark hair. Then he went with his aunt and uncle to the Seventh-day Adventist church on the sanitarium grounds.

At first it disappointed him a bit. He had never been inside a Seventh-day Adventist church in all his life. His mother had worshiped with them at home, for they lived near no church. The Lutheran churches with their fine pews and beautiful altars had provided his only experience in seeing what a church looked like; and the plain, neat pews, the quiet, simple decoration, of the Adventist church stood out in contrast.

He sensed something different about the church's atmosphere. Could it be—well—the fact it was Sabbath—the Sabbath his mother had kept? Oscar remembered such a feeling in childhood, as his gentle-speaking mother ushered in the Sabbath with her clean house and specially prepared food.

A few nurses came in, their starched uniforms gleaming in the shining pews. Then the meeting began. Someone played the organ, and they sang. Even though Oscar was not familiar with the hymns, he tried to sing. The blending of the rich voices in the lovely language of his fathers intrigued him, and the words reminded him of his mother singing as she worked around the home.

A man named Nielson gave a friendly, persuasive talk on the importance of personal decisions in the matter of ambition and life direction. He pointed out how Denmark had advanced far ahead of many other countries in democracy and social culture.

"Our social legislation assures every person born in Denmark of security," the speaker told his audience. "Nothing need deny him the necessities of life: adequate public school education, a decent home, food, clothing, and full medical care. No Dane need feel the ignominy and curse of charity. We were the first nation to pass compulsory free education laws, and the first to organize health insurance," Pastor Nielson continued.

"We were the first nation in all the world to abolish the diabolical practice of slave trading—clear back in 1798." He paused and looked searchingly at his audience.

"Yet, we are all slaves—slaves, sold under sin. We are slaves of appetite, slaves of silly habits, slaves of prejudice. We need to gather our mental forces together and make our decision as to our lifework, our future, and our destiny. Our decisions will shape our lives for time and for eternity."

Then he invited those present to give their personal testimony about decisions they had made and their consequences and results. To Oscar's utter amazement, people began to get up all over the room to speak, one by one—and their testimonies seemed to him to be small sermons. His uncle got up, and while he felt pride in the man's gentle, well-organized, impromptu speech, it filled him with a kind of terror. If everyone was supposed to talk, what in the world would *he* say? He looked about, unable to see any way he could discreetly escape. The young people present, even the most timid-appearing girls, got up with such confidence that he felt a little embarrassed at his own reluctance and fear.

"I will not shame my Uncle Ottosen," he told himself grimly. "If I'm supposed to get up and speak, I can do it if those girls can. I will just say—well, I will say how glad I am to be at Skodsborg."

But then, to his great relief, Nielson announced the closing song.

His Bible, which his old grandmother had given him at his confirmation in the Lutheran Church, came into use now. He was awkward with it at first, since he had no idea where to begin or how to find anything. But the young people of the church helped him. Before long he had sorted the Old from the New Testament, and he began to find texts for himself.

Oscar noticed a difference between the young people at Skodsborg and those around his home community. Even their conversation was different. He decided that the religion of his mother represented an entire way of life. It was like a garment worn all the time, rather than one laid aside except for certain occasions. Conversation, life, plans, all seemed to center around the church. "That's my Sabbath coat," he might hear someone say. "I don't wear it every day." Or, "What's going on at church Friday night?" "Did you see Elder -------- sleeping in prayer meeting?" "I haven't worn my hat since vespers. I must have left it at the church."

"The church, the church," Oscar thought. "Everything revolves around it. Well, that's how I remember my mother. Her religion was her life. And to Uncle Ottosen it is the same thing. He lives for his church, for his Badesanatorium—for his Lord."

CHAPTER 6

Soon after Oscar arrived at Skodsborg, a preacher named Muderspach began a series of religious meetings. He had a deep authoritative voice that attracted the young man's interest.

"Here's how you find Daniel 2," a seatmate whispered to Oscar one night during a lecture on prophecy. "It's right near the middle."

Oscar put a bookmark there, for he wanted to read it again after the meeting ended.

"Why, how did this Daniel *know* about all this, this history of the world stuff, like we heard about tonight?" he later asked one of the young men in the dormitory.

"He *didn't* know," came the reply. "God told him. God chose him to be a prophet and revealed the future to him. That's why we believe what the Bible says. It has come true."

Oscar looked at his Bible with new respect, and a little fear began to nag at him. It would awaken him in the night, and he could hear the resonance of Elder Muderspach's voice when he read, " 'In the days of these kings shall the God of heaven set up a kingdom, which shall never be destroyed.' " He fell into a kind of terror. Suppose the end of the world did come, suppose Christ should set up His kingdom before he was ready? Certainly, current events all pointed toward the possibility of vast changes in the world.

"I'm glad you like to read, Oscar," his uncle said to him once. "A wise man learns much from the wisdom of the ages." He invited him to make free use of his library. Before long he had devoured *Den Store Strid,* in English called *The Great Controversy.* He read *Aandelige Erfaringer—Early Writings*—and was delighted with *The Ministry of Healing,* which in the Danish has the title *I den Store Laeges Fodspor,* or "In the Footsteps of the Great Physician."

What he read in his uncle's books and what he saw and heard at the sanitarium—combined with his childhood Adventist experiences—began to pull him back toward the Seventh-day Adventist faith. He seriously and frequently toyed with the idea of joining the church of his mother and uncle.

But then a voice in his mind pointed out that it might be wiser to wait until after his army service before making such a decision. "It isn't logical," the voice whispered to him. "You were not an Adventist when you registered for army service. They will think it strange for a Lutheran to suddenly become an Adventist. Why don't you wait until you're through with your service, *then* take up this new religion."

At the time his mind struggled with the decision to join the Adventist faith, Oscar knew that Europe was seething. Fears and hatreds, secret treaties and a struggle for a balance of power, were tearing the Continent apart. The kaiser, for one thing, wanted to build a Berlin-to-Baghdad railroad, but the other powers in Europe did not want him to make Germany any stronger. As it was, Germany had great economic power. Tools, toys, dishes, and all kinds of manufactured goods poured out of Germany to the markets of the world. Turn over any item you might pick up in a store, and you'd see the familiar "Made in Germany."

What if, he wondered, events really began to move toward the climax that he had learned the Bible prophesied? What if a great war that might be the earth's last should explode in Europe? And what if he, Oscar, was not prepared for the spiritual consequences of such a war? What would happen to him?

Feeling that the Adventist faith was the correct and the best way to prepare for eternity, he decided to join that church. He requested and received baptism in the Ebenezer Seventh-day Adventist Church in Copenhagen.

Back on the farm, he swung into the regular routine of work again. Father did not say much about his change in religion, but Oscar lost no time in relating to Hartmann and Esther, his brother and sister at home, what he had discovered at Skodsborg.

"You were too young to remember much about our mother," he told them. "But she was right in her religion, and so is our Uncle Ottosen. Oh, you will find strange and wondrous things in the Bible. Do you know the history of the world was written down years before it happened? And that it will soon end? Great things will happen to our world, and Jesus will come, just as mother said."

Then he got his Bible, and with a skill they wondered at, he found and read Bible texts to them. Without hesitation they also accepted their mother's faith.

The time quickly drew near when he must join the army, and he felt poorly equipped to meet the new experience. Everyone had advice for him: his father, his stepmother, the hired man, even his girl friend. "Wait, Oscar, wait. Don't take up your strange beliefs until *after* you've done your stint in His Majesty's army. Why—you're in for *all* kinds of trouble."

Since he had become a vegetarian at Skodsborg, his stepmother told him he'd definitely have trouble over food. "Why, the army *marches* on *meat* for strength! They'll think you'll be ready for the insane asylum."

When his father began, "Now, son, my advice is——" Oscar knew what he was going to say. He remembered the older man's blustery opposition to his mother's gentle faith.

Even the hired man felt called upon to let him know he didn't believe such matters were really as important as Oscar seemed to think. "It would have been better if you'd never gone to the Badesanatorium. It's bound to get you into trouble. And when you get into trouble with King Christian's army, then that's trouble like you've never known before."

"They'll think it strange that when you registered for the army you were a Lutheran," his girl friend pointed out. "Now, when you're going in, you've picked up a new religion. My folks say they think it would be better if you'd wait——"

Regardless of her personal feelings, Oscar's stepmother tried hard to make his last days at home delightful without a mention of the extra work it required to cook vegetarian meals. Of course, his father had little use for the "pap diet" of the Badesanatorium. Had he not proved what great strength a pork eater can summon? He could swing a four-hundred-pound carcass or piece of one at butchering time. Then that time when the big bell at the local Lutheran church came down, he lifted it and helped put it up.

Still, despite everything, Oscar clung to his new way of life. He remembered the peace, the quiet, of the hospital and sanitarium. In his mind he could still see the nurses in snowy, crisp aprons and uniforms and smell the delicious aromas issuing from the great spotless kitchens. And the way people acted there! It all represented something to which he wanted to belong.

CHAPTER 7

War clouds were gathering in Europe. At the time Oscar entered the Danish army, the Seventh-day Adventist Church provided no medical cadet training for its draft-age young men. Nor did he know about the concept of noncombatancy in which he could participate in military duties that did not involve bearing arms. Instead, he decided not to take part in military training at all, not even the drilling and marching. Some advised him to go ahead and train and drill, but to take his stand in the event of war. But that did not seem logical to Oscar. It had to be *all* the way with him. In addition, he had the problem of Sabbath observance.

A high Adventist leader interviewed the head of the Danish War Department in Oscar's behalf, but the government official could promise little. Observing the Sabbath while serving in the army was unheard of at that time.

His girl friend, Gerda, worried about his future. She pleaded with Oscar again and again to wait and embrace his views *after* his term of service ended. It deeply bothered him that he had not managed to convert her to what he believed. Doubts began to enter his mind about his devotion to her. Would he be doing right to join his life with a girl who took lightly what he held most important? If they could not agree on matters that meant so much in his life, would it make for happiness such as he observed in his uncle's household?

Concerned about his stubbornness in regard to the observance of the seventh-day Sabbath and what trouble it might get him into, Gerda decided to go to where her handsome, dark-haired lover would enter the army. She had an aunt and an uncle in the city where he would be stationed.

"I shall go there, Oscar," she told him, shaking her hair and drooping her lashes over eyes as blue as the sea. "I think you'll need watching over." She laughed. "You'll need my advice, and I hope you'll take it."

Again the young man had a strange, lost feeling such as one feels when he is going the wrong way and is helpless to turn around.

"Of course, we must announce our engagement in the proper way," she told him aboard the train en route to the induction center. "You see, it will make it easier for me to see you. But you don't have to worry. I am not the kind of girl to chase after every man in uniform!"

It all looked logical, and Oscar was really fond of her. Yet, warning bells still kept sounding in his mind. " 'Be ye not unequally yoked together with unbelievers,' " Uncle Ottosen had said again and again. " 'Can two walk together, except they be agreed?' " he had read from the prophet Amos. Gerda was not an Adventist. They were now much more different from each other than they had been before. Again and again on his journey with Gerda, watching the landscape slip by, he seemed to see the face of his mother. Would she look with approval on his linking his life with Gerda? One of the things that had pleased him most about his baptism was the intense feeling of how happy his mother would have been. Then he reflected on her life. It had been a hard one, for, much as he loved his father, he realized now that Mr. Engen had not made it easy for her.

The engagement notices went out, as Gerda had planned, and Oscar reported for military duty on a Tuesday. The Danish army fitted and gave him a uniform, and assigned him with hundreds of others to the plain barracks. He stowed away his small possessions, tried to get used to the strange clothes, and listened for tips from his comrades and for orders from his superiors as to what he should do next.

Tuesday—not long until Friday. He continually wondered if any orders had come through about him from the War Department.

In an agony of suspense, he kept telling himself that the representatives from the local Seventh-day Adventist conference organization would do all they possibly could for him.

"Maybe the papers are lost. Maybe I've been overlooked or forgotten." He worried day and night. "It might be they think it is of little consequence—but it is life and death to me!"

In the mess hall he pushed the pork aside and ate the few vegetables, consuming much bread and butter to fill himself up.

Oscar became so concerned about his status that finally he could bear the suspense no longer. He approached his rather gruff-looking sergeant to find out if anything had come from the War Department yet.

The sergeant eyed the dark-haired young Dane in utter amazement, his mouth open in surprise. "Whoever in all the world ever heard of anything so utterly and absolutely ridiculous!" he bellowed. He finished his first loud, violent outburst with the admonition, "Don't you forget for a minute, young man, that you are in the army now, and all Europe is going to blow up one of these days. If you have a grain of sense, and know what is good for you, you'll fall in line and do as you are told. Otherwise you'll have to go see the captain."

Oscar went to his barracks that night with a feeling of terror. He tried to think of all the brave men he had ever heard of or read about.

Finally he determined to go and see the captain, even though he had a reputation as the strictest and the most harsh of all the officers in the Danish army. The soldiers under him had nicknamed him the "Lion Captain," and he lived up to his name.

Never would Oscar Engen forget the terrified bumping of his heart as he approached the captain on the parade field the next day. He had not a chance to even speak, to explain his problem.

Evidently the officer had learned about the young Adventist's situation. "What's this I hear about you, 78?" he roared, not even allowing the soldier the dignity of his name.

Politely, as respectfully as he could, Oscar attempted to explain what to him was now his most precious possession—the religious faith his mother had lived and loved. The captain continued to glare at him, occasionally clearing his throat rudely. "We believe the commandments," Oscar heard himself say, as if it were some other person talking. "One of them says not to kill. We——"

"Now, is that so!" the angry captain exploded in disgust. "Now just how could you run the Danish army on that? I never heard of such foolishness."

But Oscar went on, calmly explaining about the Sabbath and that he did not want to work or to train on that day. "I love my country," he said. "I will do other things. I will work, take care of the sick, peel potatoes, or——"

But he got no further.

"I've been looking your papers over," the officer interrupted, his face set in a mask of severity. "I find nothing said of such foolishness in the papers you filled out. Just when did you think all this up? How long have you been one of these—what-do-you-call-them—Advents?"

"My Uncle Ottosen at Skodsborg——" Oscar began.

"Never mind your uncle! How long has it been since you've gone crazy as all this?"

"I went up to Skodsborg——"

"Never mind that. How long have you been one of these Advents, which I never heard of before?"

A great calmness came over the young soldier. "About six months, sir," he answered quietly.

"So—you had not joined this, what you call the Seventh-day Advent Church, when you registered for the Danish army?"

"No, sir."

"What do you mean, then, by springing this so suddenly upon us? Didn't you know that if you changed churches, you'd get yourself in no end of trouble—especially by taking up the unheard-of belief you chose?"

"I did not think of that, sir, when I came

to believe it at Skodsborg. You see, my mother was a member of this church, and my Uncle Ottosen——"

"Why do you talk about your uncle all the time? This is *your* affair. Why didn't you use some common sense and wait until your term of army service ended instead of springing this strange request upon us?"

"Because I believe it is right, sir, with all my heart, and I think it's a matter of life and death!"

The sun boiled down while Oscar stood at attention facing the Lion.

The tall, toughly built soldier laughed harshly. "Where did you get that Saturday idea, 78? Think it up yourself?"

"Why, no, sir—it is one of the Ten Commandments. The fourth one. It says, 'Remember the——' "

"You don't need to quote it to me. I've heard it. Had to learn them when I was confirmed. But I want to ask you this: What does your father think of your outlandish way of acting?"

"He—does not like it, sir."

"I wouldn't think he would. He's probably ashamed to have you as a son. And, listen here, there's another commandment—about honoring your father and mother. I learned *it*. Now, do you call this an *honor,* for you to get yourself clapped into the guardhouse?"

Oscar remained at attention. "Sir," he said, "the Bible says that we should obey God rather than man."

The captain exploded. The red mounted up from his neck to his cheeks, to his ears; his eyes blazed. "Now, look here, 78," he shouted. "We can't run an army on the million or so ways that ignorant people interpret the Bible. Our enemies would wipe Denmark off the map. Why can't you do what most of the churches do, quit quibbling and frittering away time about minor things like what day is your Sabbath?"

By this time, they had attracted nearly everyone's attention on the parade ground, and Oscar felt conscious of many staring eyes. Again he spoke softly and calmly, "Sir, my mother's faith and belief is not a minor thing to me."

The officer stepped close to the young soldier, his face inches from Oscar's. "If you fail to obey *one* army regulation, 78," he spoke slowly and menacingly, almost in Oscar's ear, "and that goes for that preposterous Saturday business, too, we'll put you in jail. And when your parents hear about that, they'll be crying for you. Do you call *that* honor?"

"Sir, I wish you would let me tell you. My mother and my uncle——"

"Your uncle again!" he shouted. "Can't you say *anything* without dragging that everlasting uncle in? You're in trouble, and bad trouble, I tell you, 78, and a dozen uncles can't help you out when you're in trouble in the army. Now, all I've got to say is this: You line up, and line up *fast,* or I'll see to it that you are punished to the fullest extent of military law."

Then the Lion deliberately turned his back on Oscar, as if he were not worthy of any further consideration.

The young man walked slowly back to the barracks. "What now?" he asked himself. The Lion had made him realize that he could expect no mercy.

When he got to the barracks, he went in and sat on his cot. Having made his decision, he had not even a thought of turning back. Yet he was human enough to face the fierce and fiery trial with some fear. He thought of his girl friend. What would she say? What would her father and mother think of a lover who faced dishonor and disgrace?

CHAPTER 8

While he sat on his bunk, pondering, he began to wonder if God could really approve of his friendship with Gerda. It was as if he was so miserable that he might as well add a little more anguish. He buried his face in his hands, and his great mop of black hair fell over his fingers.

All of his dreams—dreams of his work on a great estate, then coming home to the neatness of a white farmhouse and the kettle singing, and the table set for tea—all of his dreams of peace could never be. Uncle Ottosen had counseled him several times in his quiet voice, " 'Be . . . not unequally yoked together' with a non-Adventist, Oscar. Find someone who believes as you do. You won't find permanent happiness in any other course."

Then Oscar prayed that if God could not bless his friendship with Gerda, He would influence her to terminate it. Even then, as he prayed, it seemed to tear at the foundations of his soul. But after a while he felt a little better, even though thoughts of her still kept flooding through his mind.

In her letters to him, and when she saw him, she had constantly advised him to give up what she considered an unwise stand. "Why don't you wait until after your army service, Oscar?" she had urged him just a few days before. "If it is as good as you say, it will wait. You got along all those years *before* without it. Oh! I wish you'd never gotten mixed up with your uncle and Skodsborg. It is going to ruin our lives, Oscar!"

Oscar had stared at her, discerning the real meaning behind her words. He knew she felt sure that if she could persuade him to wait, she might induce him afterward to forget it altogether. The thought dimmed her beauty in his eyes. His uncle and aunt's peaceful home came before his mind. Well, he would follow his convictions and see what Gerda would do. If the relationship were wrong, it would come to nothing.

It seemed to Oscar that the Minister of War, whom the Danish Adventist leaders had contacted in Oscar's behalf, must have forgotten all about the case. He recalled ruefully that the Lion captain had warned him to think things over before he took such a radical stand, which would surely get him into serious trouble.

The next day, Thursday, the officer sent him to a prominent military judge in the city of Aalborg. He knew that the army officials were attempting to persuade him to give up his stand. As he remembered the harsh and unpleasant interview with the captain, forebodings filled him while he approached the great structure which housed the offices of the well-known judge. He walked slowly up the wide steps of the ancient building and found the judge's office. The official's courteous manner and careful attention greatly relieved Oscar. The young Adventist's problem seemed to be a new one despite the man's long experience.

He stirred and sighed, and waited some time before he replied. "I am sorry you feel so deeply about your religion, young man," the white-haired judge said. "It is most unusual. You see, the army is not exactly a religious institution, and it would be hard, almost impossible, to grant concessions such as you ask to everyone who had a bit of a difference in belief."

"I realize that, sir. But what can I do, when the things I believe so strongly go in direct opposition to army routine? I love my country and my king, but my belief in obedience to God comes first."

The older man thought a moment. "What I cannot understand, Oscar, is this," he said slowly. "Why could you not have contented yourself with the Lutheran religion of your forefathers? This church does not require so many unheard-of, impossible things as the one you have so lately embraced. It seems fantastic to me."

"My Uncle Ottosen, who is the head physician at the Skodsborg Sanitarium, feels as strongly as I do on these matters, sir. I think we take our religion more seriously than other people do theirs."

"I have heard good things of Skodsborg Sanitarium," the judge observed. "But I have also heard some observe that they have narrow views on things of little importance. You would do well, my boy, to not get out of step with the whole world by following the fanaticism they seem to practice."

As Oscar stood looking at the judge's kindly face, he realized with a sinking heart that nothing he could say would make the man understand what he believed and what it meant to him.

"I will see what I can do," the judge continued, "though it is extremely irregular. I may be able to get you a couple of hours off on Saturday, perhaps between the hours of ten to twelve, so that you can attend your services. Of course we will expect you to follow the regular army routine the rest of the day. I do not even know if I can do that. You must remember you have made a most unusual request."

He appreciated the man's sympathetic manner, but Oscar knew he could not accept such a compromise. He had just as well not observe the Sabbath at all as to keep it piecemeal. He thanked the judge, but told him that God could not approve of observing the seventh-day Sabbath in such a manner.

"I wish you would think this over carefully, my son. You surely have not considered what your stand is going to cost you. The discipline in the Danish army is too rigid to permit such exceptions. You are making a terrible mistake, and you are going to bring great hardships upon yourself needlessly."

Oscar left even more depressed than when he had come. If the kindest man he had met so far could give him no hope, then how could he expect any sympathy from any other quarter? He walked slowly back to the barracks.

CHAPTER

The next day, with hundreds of others, young Oscar went to the large military drill ground some distance from the barracks. Before starting their practice, they had to stand at attention and listen to an address by their famous captain. His bearing resembled a menacing lion more than ever as he faced the group, his face grim.

"If I had been only half an inch taller," Oscar moaned to himself, "I might have been one of the King's Guard, parading daily in colorful uniform in front of beautiful Amalienborg Palace." But, no—no such good fortune was his—and now that it was Friday, he must meet his fate.

"You are now in the Danish army," the captain barked. "I want you to understand that you must unquestioningly obey any command from any of your officers." Oscar felt that the speech was for his benefit. "You must obey every command," the captain continued, "regardless of the cost to yourself or anyone concerned. This could easily mean the loss of a limb, an arm, or a leg. In fact, even if it involved death, it is still your duty to obey unquestioningly. You have homes, parents, who have sent you to be the armed strength of Denmark. We have to learn well here in this time of peace what we will have to do in time of war."

The sun burned down on the parade ground. The new recruits grew tired of standing at attention, but the captain persisted, "Regardless of what *you* think, you must do what your superiors tell you."

Finally, to their relief, the officer stopped, and their exercises began. It was hard for some of them to respond to his swift commands. He furiously attacked some who did not quite understand them, or were a little slow in responding. "When I give a command for you to run," he shouted, "I mean RUN, and as fast as you can! When I command you to halt and stand still, I don't want to see an eye moving in your head!" There followed such a strenuous drill session that some of the men blacked out. It made no difference to the captain. He wanted the men to support their comrades and obey orders. Before the day ended, each man realized that he was definitely in the army.

The Sabbath dawned for Oscar, and a more dreaded and bewildering dawning he had never experienced in all his life. The sky was as dark and overcast as seemed his prospects for the future. He arose and dressed long before the rising bell clanged. Calmly he chose his best uniform, the one he had received to wear on Sunday or when off duty.

His dress uniform elicited laughing comment from others in the barracks, though their remarks were not unkindly. They were amused at Oscar and curious as to what the outcome of his rebellion would be. "No one can beat the Lion," someone said.

When the sergeant of Oscar's company arrived, he seemed surprised. "Well, 78," he said in a brusque voice, "now, just where do you think *you* are going?"

"Sir," Oscar addressed the sergeant politely, "I told you on Tuesday that I belong to the Seventh-day Adventist Church, and that this is a day the Lord has made holy."

The noncommissioned officer stood and looked the young man up and down for some minutes. "*Well,* this young pup is up to his ears in trouble, but it's no concern of mine," he thought to himself. "If he wants it so bad, there's no one to hinder him!"

"I won't argue with you if you're so anxious for punishment," he said out loud. "But I think you better come along with the company and see the captain. It's up to him, I guess. You'll have to settle with him, and I don't envy you. I'd sooner meet up with a real lion."

Oscar agreed with him heartily—he wished himself anywhere else but on the parade ground, conspicuous in his best uniform, and headed to meet the fiercest human being it had ever been his misfortune to encounter. Then—to be shouted at and humiliated before twenty-two companies of men and their sergeants! And the bad part of it was, he was a virtual prisoner in the officer's power. Yet never for a moment did he entertain the thought of surrender.

While his company marched in formation through the city streets, his mind whirled in turmoil. When they arrived at the large parade ground, the attention of everyone seemed to focus on Oscar, standing there miserably in his best uniform. After the sergeants received their instructions from the Lion captain, each officer went to his company, and the drill began. Oscar's sergeant told him he must go and present his case to the captain.

With trembling limbs, the private stumblingly approached the officer.

The irate, red-faced captain whirled upon Oscar and began to shout orders at him in a tone that showed he expected nothing but instant and full obedience. "Look at you! In a dress uniform on the drill ground as if you were the king himself! I thought I told you three days ago just what you would do. Now get back to your company and get into line, and I mean *fast,* or you'll take the consequences."

Despite the captain's fury, Oscar stood his ground and waited politely to speak. "Sir," he said, "I told you three days ago that I cannot drill today. It is my Sabbath. I will serve my country any other way I can, but to break the Sabbath or to take lives, these I cannot do."

Infuriated, his face bloodred, the captain clenched his fists, looking as if he would like to personally flog the young private as he stood there. "You say you *can* not, 78," he bellowed. "You mean *will* not. I tell you, I have never as an army officer given the same order twice. But I see I'll have to, to a dumb ox like you. In case you have failed to consider the results of your refusal, I'm going to give you one more chance. Now, will you fall in line, or won't you?"

The stillness in the field was intense as Oscar answered, "Sir, I have already told you. I cannot." The calmness he felt surprised even himself.

The officer's rage knew no bounds. He could barely choke out an order to have Oscar locked up in the stockade.

In some ways it was a relief to Oscar to have it settled one way or the other. Soldiers seized him as if he were a dangerous criminal and took him away to a small cell. Shoved in, he heard the door click behind him. Suddenly he felt so weak that he had to sit down on the narrow cot, where he realized he would sleep also. It did not seem possible that only last week—only seven short days ago—he had been at home, wandering in the fields and looking out at the sea, keeping the Sabbath in peace and quiet. He recalled that his father had expressed concern, had asked him several times if he had made arrangements for keeping the Sabbath, and for not bearing arms in the army. Oscar had, of course, assured his father that the leaders of his church were doing all they could.

He looked around. His small cell was in an ancient building and had a stone floor and heavy iron bars at the small window. With nothing to do but sit, he wished he had his Bible, or some of his other books. At least he could pray. And he could also remember his happiness-filled six months at Skodsborg. Strange, he could think of his uncle's pear tree at such a time. His uncle had planted it as a reminder of the fruit country of Michigan, where he had spent some time at the Battle Creek Sanitarium. Everywhere Dr. Ottosen had seen orchards of pears, peaches, apples, cherries, and plums. Now Oscar's uncle tried to make the pear tree thrive at Skodsborg as a small reminder of the Michigan fruit country and his experiences there.

At first Oscar could only dimly hear other voices in the old prison. Then footsteps came softly along the stone corridor, and one of the prison guards stopped in front of the cell door. Keys rattled on a metal ring, then Oscar heard the guard insert one into the lock of his cell door. The key turned the lock with a click. Oscar sprang to his feet. Was it some new trial about to befall him? What was going to happen now?

CHAPTER

The guard spoke in a low voice, almost a whisper. "78," he said, "I just want to tell you that you are different from any man ever brought into this prison while I've been here. Oh, I've seen them brought in cursing, half drunk, and hard to manage; but you came quietly."

"Thank you, sir," Oscar replied.

"And I want to say this," the guard added, looking behind himself cautiously. "We know why you're here. I think you've got a lot of courage to stand up for what you think is right. Lots of men would have given in. You just stand up for your convictions, and I believe God will help you." Then he quietly vanished.

About the time they went through the old fortress to light the lamps, the guard slipped down to Oscar's cell. "Listen, 78," he whispered, "I had a little time today, so I went down to the pastor's house of the church where I go. I told him about your case. It's not right for you to suffer like this. He says he'll have the whole church pray for you. I don't care if you *aren't* a Lutheran! *Lutherans* were once persecuted. We mustn't make it hard for people who want to live up to what they believe. That wasn't Martin Luther's way."

After the guard left, Oscar prepared for bed. It was long after midnight before sleep came to his weary eyes. The bright sunlight lay in a square patch on the floor when he awakened to the strains of music—the military band playing in honor of the queen's birthday.

He turned sadly away from the narrow window, washed as well as he could with the limited facilities of his cell, and began another long, lonely day, filled only with his prayers and reflections. It seemed to stretch out, each second becoming an eternity.

Then Oscar remembered with a pang that it was the Sunday evening he had planned to get permission to go to the railway station to see his sister. Going through Aalborg on her way back to work from a holiday at home, she had told her brother she would look for him on the station platform since her train made a ten- or fifteen-minute stop in the city. Oscar had talked over with her some of his vague premonitions about his impending army service. "So if I am not at the station," he had concluded, "you will know I am in some kind of trouble."

The prison stood near the network of railroads that went in several directions out of

Aalborg, and he could hear the whistle of the train as it chugged into the station. He knew his sister had perhaps gotten off the train to look for him, and she would know that something had happened to him. As the sun went down, he felt more desolate than ever. He wondered wearily how long the cell would be his home.

He did not have long to find out. His court-martial convened the next day. The captain determined to make a speedy public example of the young man who had defied him.

Oscar prayed a great deal that Monday morning, and could hardly eat the breakfast a guard brought to him.

The army had offered him an attorney to help him plead his case. Perhaps he made a mistake in refusing the help, but he had been so often humiliated and rebuffed when he tried to explain his position that he thought even a lawyer might ridicule him or try to get him to soften his determination or persuade him to compromise.

That fateful Monday morning a soldier ushered him into the long courtroom. Though he knew he would not budge from his position, he could not help it that his knees were trembling.

A large table stood in the center of the courtroom, and around it sat thirteen high-ranking officers in full military dress. The military judge whom he had visited only the week before presided over the assembly.

A clerk read the list of charges against him, and Oscar noted to his amazement that the captain had added a list of other things he simply had not done. The wording of the accusations implied that Oscar was a malcontent who would obey no legitimate rule of army life, and, unless the court dealt with and made him an example, his influence would seriously threaten the morale of his whole section of the Danish army.

Oscar gasped. So the captain would actually sacrifice Oscar's life to revenge himself.

The Seventh-day Adventist Church had sent a written statement of its stand toward the military. A clerk read it before the tribunal.

Then, though worn with sleeplessness and worry, Oscar arose to defend his stand for a religious faith which he felt was worthy of even yielding up his life for. He did well, for such a recent convert. What he lacked in rhetoric, he made up in sincerity and dedication. Still he was nervous because of the consciousness of the battalion of unfriendly eyes.

In a quiet voice he told of his mother's faith and how he had found it again in the home of his mother's brother, Dr. Carl Ottosen, head physician of the sanitarium at Skodsborg. Having studied carefully under his uncle and Elder Muderspach, he could defend his belief.

Exhausted and downcast, Oscar finally sat down. The judge arose and addressed the assembled officers. He admonished them that, in the light of the evidence they had heard and of the defense of the accused, they use justice and mete out a fair sentence. All thirteen officers arose and swore an oath that they would do so.

Oscar left the room to sit in an adjoining small chamber while they deliberated. He felt more forlorn and forsaken than ever while he sat there, wondering what terrible punishment would be his. Clenching and unclenching his hands, he repeated to himself, "I *know* what I believe *is true,* and I must believe it. No matter what they do to me, they cannot destroy my faith."

Then a solemn officer opened the door, and a guard led Oscar into the room for sentencing. An officer read the punishment:

1. Oscar was to spend one month in jail, over three weeks of it in a dungeon with only bread and water. During the approximately one week spent in a regular cell, he would get prison rations. For each week spent in the dungeon, he was to have two days in a lighted cell. After the month ended, the prisoner would receive another chance to obey the military rules and comply with army discipline.

2. If Oscar caused any further trouble, the former sentence would double. If he continued

to refuse to follow military procedure, the army would automatically send him to prison for life.

3. If by any chance war should break out, he would be executed by firing squad.

The harshness of the punishment horrified him. He had not expected anything so severe. Yet when Oscar regained his composure, he still believed that in some way God would help him.

As they left the courtroom, a high-ranking officer rode up on horseback and asked how the trial came out. When told, he shouted angrily that it was not severe enough. To add insult to injury, the officer sent Oscar to the captain to tell him in person his sentence. The order added to his hardships, for the captain's quarters were a long way from the court.

Oscar and an escort set out to tramp through the long city streets to the army camp miles away just to endure the further humiliation of describing his punishment to the captain. Every step he took filled him with increasing dread.

Back at the military base, the captain listened, his face, as always—it seemed to Oscar—red with anger. "That first month is just the beginning, 78," he said the second Oscar finished his report. "You'll see plenty more, if you keep on as you have."

The sentence passed against Oscar Engen was so severe in its nature that the top officials in the War Department had to sign the order before he could start serving his sentence. His superiors suggested that he join his company and do as much as he conscientiously could until they heard from the War Department.

It took considerably longer than they had expected, so the next few Sabbaths he had no difficulty. They did not put him in jail, for that would be adding to the sentence already passed on him. Instead, they ordered him to stay in his quarters on the Sabbath. He tried in every way to comply with each order given him so as to cause no more trouble.

Gerda's letters to him had become less frequent, more strained, and not so friendly. But she was still in the city, and had not given him up entirely. Even though Oscar had qualms about her and wondered if she would ever accept his religious beliefs, he still longed for human companionship. One night he went to visit her in Aalborg. He had not seen her since his court-martial, and he wondered what she thought of it. They had much to talk about. Even though she suggested they break up their friendship, they were still deeply attracted to each other. And he tried to convince her that God would help him in some way. When he finally looked at the clock, he was horrified to see what time it was. He grabbed his hat and ran all the way back to the base. In spite of his haste, he was five minutes late. A guard let him in; the unsympathetic sergeant told Oscar about his tardiness.

Oscar's watch had just ten o'clock, but the sergeant's showed Engen was late, and army discipline is strict.

"I'm sorry, sir," Oscar said. "I was with friends and did not realize it was so late. I ran all the way back."

"Huh!" he sneered. "You refuse to do anything on Saturday. Now you come in late from your leave."

Oscar did not expect him to report such a minor infringement to the captain, but he did, and the officer was furious.

"You're a great one," the captain exploded. "You're so religious you won't participate in military training, but what's wrong with getting into the barracks when you're ordered to do so? Is that against your religion, too? This unwarranted tardiness will go into your report to the War Department and will no doubt add to your penalty."

Oscar received a copy of the report which the Lion carefully wrote out about Engen's tardiness, and, to his dismay, he saw that the captain had played it up big. "Private Oscar Engen has not only refused to participate in military training on Saturday, but transgresses the rules and regulations in regard to being present in his quarters at night." The captain made it appear that it was a regular occurrence.

Oscar realized with sinking heart that the odds were stacked against him.

The stand of the young soldier had reached the papers and had stirred the whole city. Many sympathized with him, but others regarded it as a lot of fuss over an unimportant matter. His relationship with his girl friend had grown somewhat strained anyway, and the news of Oscar's disgrace and court-martial almost brought things to a climax. All of Gerda's relatives and friends urged her to have nothing further to do with him.

On the night that he had gone to see her—the night he returned late to the barracks—he had told her that with all of the opposition of her relatives, he did not want to bring any hardship and disgrace upon her. It was impossible not to note the family's frigid attitude when he went to see her. Earlier they had welcomed him with open arms. But now they had forgotten the rich acres of his father's farm and the dozens of head of stock. They could see only his court-martial and disgrace.

Gerda still remained faithful to him despite the opposition of her family, which touched Oscar's heart. If ever he needed a friend, it was now. And he believed that if God saved him from the sentence of the court-martial, she would see things as he viewed them. The fact that she did not call him foolish or fanatical kept his hope alive.

Yet she continued to tell Oscar that she thought it would be wiser to put off being an Adventist until after his military service. "My family says that is the least you can do for your country, Oscar! Why, my father remembers when we lost all of Schleswig-Holstein to the Germans in the 1860's. People have said if our army had been stronger—— My parents say you ought to do that much for me, if I am willing to accept you with the peculiarities of your uncle's religion."

It did sound logical. If he continued on the course he had chosen, it seemed inevitable that he would get sentenced for life to the government penitentiary. Then what would happen to their plans for the future?

If he would, as she suggested, submit to military authority, then in two years he could take up his beliefs again, they would get married, and all of their plans for the future could come true. Then he could walk with her by the seashore and show her how lovely and peaceful the Sabbath always was at Skodsborg. She almost convinced him—almost!

When he lay down on his narrow cot, the dream would fade away, and he could see in memory his mother's face. "I can't, I can't, I can't," he would groan, and his determination to stand firm to his faith would grow stronger than ever.

At the same time that Gerda was pressuring

him almost beyond his endurance, a letter came to him in his father's handwriting. His father reminded him that he had never wanted him to go visit his uncle in the first place, and that all of his trouble had come upon him because he had let the man unduly influence him in a way that would ruin Oscar's life. Not only that, the disgrace hurt his whole circle of relatives and friends. The local Lutheran pastor had said that the Holy Scriptures declared that men should subject themselves to the higher powers, for God had ordained or authorized them. His father advised him to obey governmental authority in its domain, and to obey God in His area. It really seemed to him, and to those who advised him, that when a person joins the army, it is his duty under God to go along with the army.

The letter did not convince Oscar. Nor did it encourage him. It seemed as if the whole world opposed him. He needed encouragement such as the unknown guard in the prison had given him. The dread of the court-martial and the fear of hard labor and the hardships of imprisonment in the government penitentiary were not nearly so hard to bear as the reproach and the pleading of his relatives. "Don't go through with it, Oscar!" they said. "You can avoid it! Only two years. Then you are on your own and can do as you please. Do you want to spend the rest of your life in prison? If you don't care for yourself, then what about us? What are you *doing to us?*" They all gave him the same advice, but Oscar sensed that if he went against his conscience, he might never regain his faith. It seemed as if he had reached a point of "no return."

If he drifted away from Sabbath observance and from the other principles he had learned at Skodsborg during his army life, he doubted if he would ever return. He felt as if the presence of the Holy Spirit would leave him forever.

CHAPTER

Now he faced his darkest hour. Standing alone, without a word of kindness or encouragement from anyone, it seemed as if he could not bear to go on. The load pressed so heavy that he began to pray for God to somehow forgive him if unbearable circumstances forced him to lay aside his religious faith for the short time he served in the army. Surely God would forgive him in such terrible circumstances, when his liberty, his life, and his happiness were all at stake. A man has only one life, after all.

Then it seemed as if, out of the mental darkness that surrounded him, a voice spoke to him. "Do you realize that if *you* cannot stand for God and what you believe in this ordeal, what of others who will follow you? Certainly other young men will decide to keep the commandments of God. If *you* fail God now, you will be making it harder for others to stand for the right. Your example will weaken their faith."

Little did Oscar realize how many hundreds of people were watching the outcome of his brush with military authority on the subject of conscientious objector status. How carefree he had been when his uncle had expressed his fear about the outcome of the stand his nephew felt he should take. And the older man's fear had come true. It offered small comfort to Oscar that he was the first young Dane to take a public stand for Sabbath observance. In fact, he might even have to give up his life for his stand. The thought filled his heart with greater fear. He was young, and had looked forward with pleasure to a good and fruitful life.

He had his *Great Controversy* now, and he read it continually during the trying weeks of waiting. In it he read, "The season of distress and anguish before us will require a faith that can endure weariness, delay, and hunger—a faith that will not faint, though severely tried. . . . All who will lay hold of God's promises, as he [Jacob] did, and be as earnest and persevering as he was, will succeed as he succeeded. Those who are unwilling to deny self, to agonize before God, to pray long and earnestly for His blessing, will not obtain it."—P. 621. "The beloved of God pass weary days, bound in chains, shut in by prison bars, sentenced to be slain, some apparently left to die of starvation in dark and loathsome dungeons. No human ear is open to hear their moans; no human hand is ready to lend them help."—P. 626.

These passages especially appealed to him. Never had he felt so alone, yet a holy joy began to fill his heart, for now he knew, come what may, that he would stand, even though he must yield up his life. In his heart he knew that God watched him and would work things out to His honor, which gave Oscar a strange satisfaction not understandable to one who had never had every position of his faith severely criticized.

At the same time his relationship with Gerda had grown steadily worse. Then came the letter he had half expected for some time. "You want to be true to your religion," she wrote. "I want to be true to mine. We had better part."

Oscar had long known that a young man working on a large estate was also interested in her. "He will probably marry her and take her to America," he mused. "It is just as well. I have my troubles to attend to anyway."

The days and weeks crawled by until one afternoon—like an explosion—a telegram came from the War Department instructing those in charge of Oscar to send him to Copenhagen. They would deal with his case there.

Oscar received the news with mixed feelings. In Aalborg he knew what faced him. But if they treated him so harshly here, might they not be even more severe in far-off Copenhagen?

Still it would be a great relief to get away from the army officers at Aalborg, who, with only one or two exceptions, had continually made his life a burden. He was particularly glad to see the last of the Lion. Surely no one in Copenhagen could be worse than he! And the chances were, at least, he might find more sympathetic treatment. It came to Oscar that the new development was an answer to his prayers. He prepared for his journey from the north of Jutland, across the island of Funen, then by sea to the island of Zealand—and Copenhagen. It also comforted him to know that he would be near Skodsborg.

The train ride was a long one, though interesting. Oscar loved his wonderful country. The train took him south to Aarhus, an ancient town. He had visited there in better days and had seen some of its quays, and the Old Aarhus Cathedral, built in 1200.

He wished he could leave the train at the once-walled city of Fredericia. Not far from there, at Jelling, still exist great runic stones from the tenth century, commemorating King Gorm and Queen Thyra. Ancient burial mounds huddle on either side of the village church, which some claim to be the oldest Christian structure in all of Scandinavia. But Oscar could not stop—he had to go on.

After many weary hours, he reached the

island of Zealand. Some time before he got to Copenhagen, the train steamed into the city of Roskilde, which until 1444 was the capital of Denmark. It is an ancient city, and all Danes delight in its history. Oscar knew that some forty or more Danish kings lie buried in its brick cathedral, including the famed Christian IV, who built so much of Copenhagen.

As the train jolted along, Oscar had plenty of time to think of all that had happened to him in the past few weeks. He could have postponed his going into the army a short time longer. That might have been better. But if war threatened the nation then, it could have been worse. The army would have been less likely to grant him any special privileges.

Or, if he had done as hundreds of other Scandinavians had done, he could have left for America. Then he could have skipped his compulsory military training altogether. Anyway, it was too late to conjecture on what might have been. Most certainly if he had known of all the anguish he would have to endure, and of the severity of his court-martial sentence, he would have even now been on his way to America. But perhaps God had allowed it to happen to him to make military life easier for some other person.

One thing, he thought a bit ruefully, the whole episode had brought seventh-day Sabbath observance to the attention of the whole Danish army. Not only the army knew of the conflict of one lone Seventh-day Adventist recruit, but the whole country. The newspapers all over Denmark had carried the story in one way or another. The question that now faced him was, What will happen next?

CHAPTER 12

After the train arrived in Copenhagen, Oscar gathered his things together and went, as ordered, to a large military academy. As he walked to the training school for officers, he looked at the city around him. He smiled to see the Borsen, or Exchange, a building with a spire shaped like four dragons whose tails twine up to a peak. Nearby was Amalienborg, with four palaces set around a great open square, one of them the king's palace.

He went on, swinging along the old streets, wondering what the next few hours would hold for him. Grimly he smiled when he recalled that even the encyclopedia, in speaking of the religion of his country, said that while the state religion was Lutheran, the nation had complete religious freedom for all faiths. "That doesn't mean in the *army*," he decided.

At Aalborg he had had no trouble with the common soldiers. They had been pleasant to him even in his trouble. It had been the officers who had given him trouble, and he now feared the ones he would encounter here at the military academy. However, to his surprise and relief, he learned the officers in Copenhagen were just the opposite.

The officers treated him with kindness and respect, and without exception were as pleasant a group of men as anyone would want to serve under. But the common soldiers! He discovered that they had come from the lowest strata of society. Many of them were criminals and ex-convicts. Oscar understood that the army had sent them to the academy, where there were more officers than enlisted men, so that it could deal with them in case any of them got out of hand.

Plainly the army had transferred Oscar here to classify him with the group of criminals. Some of his superiors had evidently depicted him to the authorities of the War Department as a serious offender.

As Oscar turned into the grounds, a soldier ran up to him and, giving a glance at the number on his uniform, asked in a patronizing tone, "Well, what have *you* done that they've sent you here? Me, I didn't do much—it was just a little chestnut stand—the old lady yelled like crazy, and, well, here *I* am with a bunch of rogues."

Oscar had never met anyone before who seemed to take it for granted that he was a criminal. "I didn't break any law or do anything like that," he told him. "I—I—just observe a different day from Sunday. I keep Saturday, and I cannot drill or work on that day. It is against my religious belief."

A knot of soldiers nearby had evidently sent the questioner to get information on the newcomer. The soldier stood and looked at Oscar for a moment as if he could not believe what he had just heard. "What did you say?"

Oscar repeated his problem, saying it was only a mix-up in regard to his day of worship—not any crime, or infringement of civil law.

The tough-faced soldier guffawed loudly, as if Oscar had said the most unbelievably funny thing he had ever heard. He whirled about and in a loud, coarse voice informed his friends that here was a great donkey who had gotten mixed up in his head. He had some crazy notion about going to church on Saturday instead of the Sunday civilized people kept.

Engen continued on to the academy's headquarters building. There he presented his papers, and a secretary ushered him into the presence of the military commander of the school. A gray-haired man with a pleasant face, he told Oscar to have a seat. The official looked at Oscar's papers, then opened a folder. Examining Oscar with a kindly smile, he said, "I understand by your report, Mr. Engen, that you have been sent to us because of your religious convictions, which seem to have gotten you into considerable difficulty in your army camp in Jutland."

"Yes, sir; that is correct, sir."

The officer smiled at him again. "It seems that you are very persistent in wishing to follow your convictions."

"Why, yes, sir."

"If you will likewise be equally true to the principles and rules of this school, you will get along fine, and you will have no problems at all while you are with us. We do not anticipate any trouble at all from you, Mr. Engen."

Amazed, Oscar could not find an answer adequate to the occasion.

"You see, Mr. Engen, for such a sentence as the court-martial in Aalborg passed on you, they cannot enforce so severe a penalty against any soldier without the signature of the king himself. King Frederick VIII has pardoned you, and you do not have to serve the sentence at all. He has instructed us to give you the Sabbath off so that you may worship according to the dictates of your own conscience. Denmark has freedom of worship for all faiths."

Oscar felt like leaping up in the air and shouting for joy. He wanted all Copenhagen to know. He wished he could shout it so that they could hear it at Skodsborg—yes, and Aalborg, and Frederikshavn, too. With tears in his eyes and in his voice, but with a face wreathed in smiles, he arose and thanked the officer again and again.

He later learned that when his sentence had reached the Minister of War for his needed signature, the man became suspicious at the charges—which seemed so minimal—and searched the papers for evidence of crimes terrible enough to warrant such a punishment. The whole affair puzzled him. He could find no evidence that Oscar Engen was a hardened criminal. Finally, he took Oscar's papers to King Frederick VIII and secured a complete pardon.

The commanding officer sent the young soldier to one of the junior officers for his assignment. Again, Oscar did not have to explain anything. The younger officer already had heard about his case.

"Since you are keeping the seventh-day Sabbath, you must be a Seventh-day Adventist," he commented to Oscar.

Oscar smiled his assent. It was good to smile and be able to talk to people without having to weigh every word he said.

"We have all heard of Skodsborg, and I take it for granted that you are a man accustomed to your morning and evening prayers. I realize that you would hardly fit in with the type of men we have here. Now I am not sure I can do this, but if I can arrange it, would you like to have a room to yourself?"

"I would appreciate that more than I can

tell you," Oscar replied, remembering the encounter with some of the soldiers before he entered the building.

Somewhat later the officer led him to a plainly furnished but comfortable room. It was not luxurious, yet it was a palace compared to what he might have had to endure if God had not worked out things for him.

"This is going to be your home as long as you are with us," the other man told him.

In the room Oscar could keep his Bible, *The Great Controversy, The Ministry of Healing,* and all of his writing paper, notebooks, and stamps. Naturally neat, he appreciated having a chest in which to put his belongings. He realized as he unpacked that the quiet room would be much safer for him than the general sleeping quarters.

The private room was a source of jealousy among the enlisted men at the academy. "Why should this newcomer be so favored?" they asked one another angrily. "Here he receives a room as good as those assigned to the junior officers. Who does he think *he* is, anyway? We heard that he came to the academy because of some trouble he'd gotten into, yet you'd think he was a relative of the king himself."

Oscar's room stood at the end of a long hallway. He kept it locked even while he was in there resting or reading. Often he heard a number of men congregate outside his door and remark about him in insulting terms, telling what they'd like to do with him. Sometimes, late at night, Oscar would awaken to hear rough hands trying the door, voices muttering angrily.

Instead of spending his days drilling and trying to explain why he could not conscientiously bear arms, Oscar had familiar tasks to do. He watered, fed, and saddled the officers' horses. Every officer had about five horses, each of which someone took out from forty-five minutes to an hour a day. The officer cadets had intensive horsemanship training, such as learning to jump the sleek animals over obstacles and fortifications of all kinds. The groomsmen-soldiers fed and watered the horses three times a day.

It aroused real anger and jealousy among the other enlisted men that Oscar had a whole day off from his work. While it was not hard work, his superiors still excused him on the Sabbath and asked no questions. The other men received no such consideration. They had to take care of the animals the same on Sunday as on any other day. Oscar worked with them on Sunday and had the benefit of all their slurring remarks and innuendos. He said nothing in reply, reflecting that even their insults were much more pleasant than what he had endured before. He realized the jealousy and animosity some held toward him, so he went out of his way to be especially kind and considerate. After work the other enlisted men often went into town to drink, or worse.

One day, as Oscar was leaving the stable, he heard two of them talking. One of them had particularly complained about Oscar's special treatment. He overheard one of them say they planned to kill someone before the day ended, that there'd be one less—and they garnished the epithet with choice vulgarities—prancing around day after day to offend people.

Oscar felt sure, from their glances, that they were referring to him. At first he paid little heed to their loud threats, having grown used to their constant profanity. But when he realized that night was his turn for guard duty, he began to take the threat a little more seriously. They would have more opportunity to carry it out.

The large double gates at the entrance to the academy were electrically controlled up till midnight. The guard, on duty in an adjoining office, pushed a button when someone rang the bell, and the gates would swing open. At midnight the office closed, and the guard on duty had to march back and forth in front of the gate until morning.

Oscar was about to take his post outside the gate for the long night vigil, when at three minutes till twelve the gate bell jangled. Startled, Oscar pushed the button just as he was opening the door to begin his guard duty.

When the doors swung open, the two soldiers who had earlier threatened him rushed through the gates with drawn sabers. Obviously drunk, they were bound to hurt someone. Horrified, Oscar saw them attack two junior officers, and he saw the officers run out of sight into the building, shouting. Later he learned that one officer fled through a door for protection just as his pursuer raised his saber to slash him. The door slammed, and the sword bounded back and slashed the drunken assailant in his forehead. Shortly an ambulance came and carried one would-be murderer to the hospital, and soldiers took the other to prison. Oscar shuddered as he realized that the two sabers had actually been meant for him. Under the bright stars that night the young soldier had one more reason to thank the Lord for His continuous care. If the men had arrived four minutes later, they would have pinned him to the gate with their weapons.

Army life went by happily, with Oscar constantly aware of God's protection. But his experience had its effect.

By the time he had visited with his uncle at Skodsborg many times, he knew he could not marry out of his religious faith. And he knew now that he must go to America. Letters and news had come back from friends and relatives telling about its wonders. The New

World offered many more opportunities for advancement than the Old World. Even common people managed and often owned farms of many acres. People had better clothing and more food.

Oscar's uncle often commented about the abundance of fruit in America. "It is even better than Holland for fruit," he exclaimed one time, "and the country is so big that they can grow even tropical fruits in the South.

"The United States has a state called Wisconsin and one named Minnesota. Many Scandinavians have settled there, and the Adventist Church has a Danish-Norwegian college in Minnesota."

Uncle Ottosen's knowledge of America amazed Oscar.

"We have a Swedish seminary near Chicago, called Broadview," the older man continued. "You'll want to visit there. They have a farm and raise most of the fruits and vegetables the school uses."

After listening to the accounts of life in the United States his uncle and others gave, Oscar decided to go there. Naturally, his father was sorry but not surprised. Literally thousands of people jammed the ships to America. Whole families sold their homes and possessions and glutted every ship that steamed or sailed westward.

Time passed. After his service in the army

terminated, Oscar had to his intense satisfaction an honorable discharge. His superiors in the military academy at Copenhagen had been pleased with his good character, his willingness to work, and his acceptance of responsibility. They commended him for his excellent behavior, and he knew it was in marked contrast to the other men with whom he had shared his lot.

CHAPTER 13

After Oscar went up to Skodsborg and then on to his windswept farm home in Jutland to bid his last farewell, he set sail jubilantly. He did not realize that in only a few days his adventure would take on another hue—that he would wish himself back on solid ground.

In all of his sailing out to sea on skiffs and barks of all kinds up in Jutland, he had learned little about seasickness. He had balanced gleefully on homemade rafts, pitching out in the cold, boiling waters of the Kattegat, where on clear days you could almost see the dim outlines of Göteborg, over in Sweden. And he thought that as a Nordic, as one practically born on the ebb and flow of the tide, he surely would not experience seasickness.

Gaily he stowed away his belongings in the cabin and went briskly up onto the deck. To say he was in high spirits would have been an understatement. He was on the high tide of ambition, adventure, and anticipation. Of course, looking back, he had feelings of sadness. Gerda had yielded to the harassment of her relatives and had given him up, even before she had time to learn of his pardon from King Frederick himself.

Off in the dunes stood the ancient church where his mother lay sleeping, awaiting the call of Him who broke the bands of the tomb. And nearby lived his father, growing old, frustrated, and disappointed. He had been proud of Oscar's release and pardon, yet broken when he learned of the soon-coming separation. He and Oscar both knew that he, too, would be all too soon sleeping in the churchyard. Already Oscar's sister had gone to America. Her glowing letters told not only of fantastic opportunities in America, but of the bigness, richness, and efficiency of the church to which they both now belonged.

The Seventh-day Adventist Church had recently established a sanitarium, a college, and a publishing house near the nation's Capitol on the east coast of America, though what state it was in, he couldn't possibly remember—probably that California he'd heard so much about. His sister wrote about the hundreds and hundreds of opportunities one had almost for the taking.

Oscar walked about the deck, exhilarated by the brisk, cool sea breezes, delighted with his prospects, and thankful that the dark clouds which had hung so long over his life and destiny had dissipated. The Lion—why, he didn't even need to think of him, much less dread him. He wondered who cowered now in the prison cell in the old bastion where he had spent hours of humiliation and anguish.

And he felt sorry for the few people he saw who were already seasick. He saw some of them staggering about the decks, their mouths sagging, their faces greenish or white. In his superiority over their weakness, he remembered that he had read up on seasickness, just in case. The possibility seemed *remote* that he actually might have a touch of *mal de mer*. A book his uncle owned had said it was a disagreeable illness that often comes with the pitching and rolling of the sea. Dizziness, headache, nausea, a sinking feeling in the stomach, and vomiting accompany it.

Several people had advised him what to do if he got it. Take seasick pills, some said. Eat dry crackers. Drink whiskey. Don't eat anything. Don't drink anything. Eat everything. Drink copiously. Lie in bed all the time. Don't watch the sea. Oscar smiled. Such remedies were all right for those who needed them, but he was getting along just fine. He slept and ate well until one morning the liner steamed into the port of Christiania (now called Oslo).

His boat traveled up the nearly eighty miles of the Oslofjord, dotted with lovely tree-covered islands. When they reached the nine-hundred-year-old city, capital of Norway, he could see the Akershus Castle, ancient and impregnable, from the ship.

From the ancient port the ship began its long trip across the Atlantic. The Scandinavian ship was named, strangely enough, *The United States*. Oscar bought a third-class ticket, feeling sorry for the poor people crowded into the lower decks, called steerage. They were near the exhaust fumes of the engines, and often rats and bilge water got into their miserable accommodations. The liner, with its many hundreds of human beings, threaded its way back through the Oslofjord, across the Skagerrak, and on into the rough, cold waters of the North Sea on its great lumbering way to the North Atlantic. She passed to the north of Scotland near the Shetland and Orkney islands.

But Oscar, for all of his self-confidence, began feeling some strange symptoms. First he became dizzy and had a terrible headache. Suddenly, he became violently nauseated. He decided it must have been something he had eaten. Maybe he had gotten poisoned. After all, the food wasn't as—but he got no further. With staggering legs he ran to the railing, where he, with several others, became occupied for a time, vomiting. Could it be that he, Oscar Engen, used to the sea all his life, was *seasick?* He went down and crawled miserably into his bunk. Someone came in eating something. Oscar begged him to leave. The sight of anyone eating put him in anguish.

Oscar had read that seasickness is seldom if ever fatal, yet he firmly believed as he lay on the bunk in his cabin, vomiting almost continuously, that his case would be a notable exception. He could almost see the headlines in Copenhagen and Frederikshavn, "YOUNG SOLDIER PARDONED BY KING FREDERICK VIII DIES AT SEA." It gave him a kind of mournful satisfaction to think of the stir it would make at home. It would delight his former captain and the toughs at the military academy. But father would be sad, and Aunt and Uncle Ottosen would grieve. And Anna would wait for him at the docks, only to hear the mournful news, "Sorry, Miss Engen, but we had to bury your brother at sea. Yes, a sad case. But we couldn't help it. He died of seasickness."

A few trickles of tears meandered down his cheeks when he contemplated the reaction his death would make. By now he was *certain* he would die. He retched even when he didn't have anything in his stomach. For two long weeks he could get down only a bit of oatmeal.

He slept only in snatches, and that miserably and feverishly. Once in his sleep he cried out, "Let me off! I've got to get off." He awoke and saw the ship nurse standing there.

"You must get up, Mr. Engen. You'll feel better if you do," she said in a quiet voice.

"No, no!" he exclaimed with a violent retch. "No, I can't stand it! No, don't make me get up. Oh, if I'd only had the sense to stay in Denmark where I belong!"

"Mr. Engen," the nurse persisted, "you're going to have to get out of bed, or we will *make* you. You will never get well if you stay here. Do you want us to throw you overboard?"

"I don't care if you do," he groaned. "Only let me alone!"

The two weeks dragged to an end, and the sea became calmer. Oscar finally staggered out onto the deck.

"Ah," one of the passengers said, recognizing him. "You're the man who boarded at Christiania, aren't you? And you said you didn't get seasick."

Oscar turned and walked in the other direction, a little angry at the burst of laughter.

Someone cried out that he saw lights twinkling in the west. New York Harbor, someone told him. It would not be long until he could feel land under his feet. Though his legs felt like boiled macaroni, he eagerly gripped the rail, watching as the lights grew brighter.

CHAPTER 14

Presently, after what seemed hours, tugs nudged the great liner up to her pier near Ellis Island, where immigrants had to go through the formalities of entering the United States of America. After he finished with the officials on Ellis Island, he went with many others to Manhattan and one of the two huge railroad stations. Immigration was big business and well organized in those days, and his papers even indicated which one of the many immigrant trains he needed to take to go to the place indicated. His uncle, knowing how confused and lost he would be because of ignorance of the language, customs, and geography of his newly chosen home, had found him a place with a Danish farmer in Ringsted, Iowa, where he could work for a while. With much satisfaction he settled himself on one of the dusty plush seats of the railroad coach and prepared to enjoy transportation without the agonizing nausea he had suffered during his ocean voyage.

The immigrants received lunch parcels calculated to last the passenger to his destination. Then a man went through the train, laying a pound box of cheap chocolates in each person's lap. Oscar did not know what to make of such generosity, but he recalled the reputation of the United States for wealth and concluded that the candy must be a gift to welcome the weary travelers.

Hungry from his two-week fast on shipboard, he thought he would open the box and see what the railroad company had given him. He looked about and saw others opening their boxes, so he yielded to his curiosity and found two trays of chocolate creams, each nested in a small crinkled paper nest, like brown eggs laid by a candy bird. Cautiously he popped one in his mouth.

He was nearly through when the train drummer came through and demanded pay. Oscar was not the only one dismayed. People all over the immigrant coach reluctantly gave up limp dollar bills from their scant store for the box of candy, possibly worth ten or fifteen cents. Oscar comforted himself that it had not cost him more than one dollar to learn one of his first lessons in his new country.

When a fruit vendor came through, he cautiously found out prices before he took anything. He did make one bad bargain, though. Having heard in Denmark of a fruit called the banana, he chose a small coin from his coin purse and bought one just to see what people liked about it. But he soon threw it out the window, for when he tried to eat the long stringy pieces wrapped cunningly about an entirely too-large seed, he found it unpalatable.

The next day the train reached the great railroad hub of Chicago. Oscar's papers indicated that he must change trains. Since his trunk would get transferred automatically, all he had to take care of were his coats, hat, and hand luggage. He showed his paper of directions to the passenger agent, who fortunately was patient and accommodating. He showed travel-weary Oscar where he would find the train for Des Moines and indicated on his watch just when he would have to be there to board it.

Realizing he had a little time to wait, he went out of the busy station onto the streets. The traffic and confusion bewildered him, so he remained fairly near the station.

Wandering along the street, he came to a big bakery, where the smell of baking bread made him ravenously hungry. To his delight, the clerks seemed to understand him. Seeing some Danish cheeses, he bought one and a sack of hot buns and went back to the station. With his pocket knife, he opened the buns and sliced the pale cheese into their puffy hot centers.

Before he got on the train, he saw a barbershop. The large sign advertised haircuts for a quarter—a coin which he had learned—so he decided to have his shaggy hair trimmed before he arrived at his new home. He pointed to the sign, and the barber nodded. After the haircut, the barber inquired, "Would you like a tonic massage?"

Oscar, not knowing in the least what he said, replied, "Yah." The man lowered him again into the chair and rubbed an oily perfume gently into his scalp.

"Now, this *is* something," Oscar thought. "This is wonderful for a quarter." He decided he had never seen a more obliging kind of person than an American barber.

"Do you want a singe? It's good for the ends of your hair," the barber pursued.

Again the delighted young man answered, "Yah."

"Now, how about a shave and neck clipping?" the barber asked when he finished.

Once more Oscar submitted. When the barber removed the sheet, Oscar got out his long change purse, sorted out a quarter, and laid it in the smiling barber's outstretched hand.

"No, no," the man exclaimed irritably. "Not twenty-five cents for a haircut, a tonic, a singe, a shave, and a neck clip! Two dollars!"

Oscar did not know how to protest, for he did not understand the angry words the barber shouted. All he could grasp was "two dollars." He paid, and went a little chastened, poorer but wiser, to his train. One thing he had learned the hard way. Even in rich America, people did not give things away for nothing. And he seemed to be easy prey with his Old-World-style clothes, his Danish luggage, and his utter inability to understand the bewildering jargon of unintelligible sounds called the English language. Discouragement began to fill him.

He determined to be careful of the small store of money he had in his thin wallet. But when he walked over to the track where his train stood amid clouds of steam, he saw a boy selling sandwiches. Cautiously he inquired the price. Already he had eaten the rolls and cheese, and the banana had proved most unsatisfactory.

The price was not out of line, so he bought three of the sandwiches and carried them into the train with him. He forgot to ask about their contents. But when he had opened the first packet, he held the morsel up and examined it closely. A familiar-looking pinkish slice of meat hung out like ruffles all the way around. His nose informed him correctly of what he had just purchased. Ham! Ham sandwiches! And he had just wasted another two of his American quarters. Opening the window, he threw the sandwiches out in disgust.

He had grown quite hungry by the time he

got wearily off the Chicago and Northwestern train in Ringsted, Iowa. His grinning countryman, Mr. Hansen, met him with a resounding smack on the back and a hearty greeting in the Danish language. Oscar hadn't heard anything so utterly wonderful since he left Copenhagen. He climbed into the wagon beside his new friend, and they drove out of the little town, each one talking as hard as he could in their beloved Danish language.

CHAPTER 15

It was getting dusk when the horse turned into the lane of a typical Iowa farm. The two-story building, built square, with a porch on the side and the front, sat back from the road. A fence surrounded the yard. Rockers sat on the porches as if the Hansens had a lot of leisure time and could sit out there and look at the people who went by on the road.

He could see two big barns and a tool and implement shed. Many cattle crowded along the pasture fence. Impressed, Oscar decided that Hansen must have gotten quite rich—and he had not been in America long at that. He must have been more clever than Oscar, who had wasted money on haircuts and singes, cheap candy, and ham sandwiches. He could see that if he wanted to get anywhere in life, he'd have to keep his wits about him better than he had so far.

After they entered the big comfortable home, the Hansens took him to a large bedroom off the sitting room. The bed had a high wooden headboard and fat pillows. A washstand held a large pitcher and bowl decorated with pictures of rose bouquets. A piece of soap lay on a dish that matched the pitcher and bowl.

Ingrain carpeting, with a continuous pattern of rolling curlicues in dark and light green, covered the floor. A rocker with a fat brown cushion stood by the window. Oscar surveyed his new domain with deep satisfaction. Yes, indeed, Mr. Hansen was rich. After washing his hands in the big bowl, Oscar looked at the bed longingly. He hadn't stretched out to sleep for several days. He got out his key and opened his small trunk. But just then Mr. Hansen called him to supper.

Even though some of the food was strange, Oscar found it delicious. And the talk! The Hansens were eager to hear of his army experiences.

"How was your sea voyage?" Mr. Hansen asked after Oscar finished telling about his army life.

From the look on his face, his host did not need an answer. Mr. Hansen laughed so uproariously that it almost offended Oscar. The intense anguish was too recent to seem even remotely amusing. Fortunately, they changed the subject. He didn't want to remember his ocean voyage ever again if he could help it.

He spent six months in Ringsted with the Hansens, though he did not approve of the fact that the man raised hogs. When he remarked to him about it, Mr. Hansen, a Seventh-day Adventist, told him he thought it was all right to sell them to nonchurch members. Oscar decided to find other work as soon as the opportunity showed itself. Another thing that discouraged him was that he had not made any headway toward learning English. Those on the farm spoke only Danish, and he felt he was more than wasting his time there.

He saved most of his wages. About six months after he arrived in America, he got a letter from his sister in Washington, D.C. Anna told him that she had been working there as secretary to Arthur G. Daniells, president of the General Conference of Seventh-day Adventists. Up to then Oscar had been thinking strongly of moving to Washington, D.C. He had gotten acquainted with the two Dr. Kresses while they were in Skodsborg, and he felt sure that they might help him find a job. They worked at the Adventist medical institution near the nation's Capitol.

"Don't come to Washington, D.C.," his sister's letter said. "Go to Loma Linda in California. I'm going out there. They have all kinds of fine opportunities out there for people willing to work."

Oscar bade good-bye to his kind friends

the Hansens. They had been kind to him and had helped him in many ways. He had gone to church and to town with them, but he had actually lived a Danish life in America. That was not what he wanted. He still had the handicap of not knowing English. If he had worked for a little while in an English-speaking home, he would have picked up some of the language. But he had fallen into the easy habit of speaking Danish with his friend. If he were to carve out his niche in America, he must learn the English language. And he must start immediately.

He took his savings, went to the station, and bought himself a ticket to a place as near Loma Linda as the stationmaster could find. He learned he would have to change trains in Omaha, Nebraska.

Because of a mix-up, Oscar spent twenty-four hours in Omaha, desperately trying to find out what train he should take to the West. He approached every train parked in the station and held out his ticket to dozens of traffic agents, only to get waved back. Hungry and tired, he began to wonder if he would have to spend the rest of his life in Omaha, Nebraska.

Finally he went behind a heap of boxes and asked God to help him. At long last he found the right train, and a conductor took his long ticket and punched it. He stumbled into a car, sank down onto one of the faded plush seats of the Union Pacific coach, and dropped off to sleep. While he slept from utter exhaustion, the train steamed and smoked its way across plain and mountain toward Utah.

Soon the train drew into the station at Salt Lake City, and Oscar knew that this was the location of the great Mormon Temple. When he learned that the train would remain in the Salt Lake City station about two hours, he decided to walk to the Temple area to see all the sights he could. Before he left the train, the conductor managed to get him to understand that Oscar had better not return late, or the train would go off and leave him.

He got to the Temple, looked around, and headed back in the direction of the train station—he thought. "Now, I've done it," he told himself in disgust as he realized he had gone in the wrong direction. "Now what am I going to do?" He quietly prayed right on the street. Opening his eyes, he spied a policeman swinging along just ahead of him. Hastening his steps, he caught up and repeated, "Train! Train! California!" The big ruddy-faced policeman smiled and answered him in Swedish. In a few minutes Oscar boarded his train, and it chugged across the desert and mountains.

After many hours, weary and jaded, he got of at Colton, California. His eyes sparkled at the sight of orange groves and the fruit lying all over the ground. Oranges were so costly in

Denmark that the people had them only for special holidays.

Although he had no idea how to get to Loma Linda from the station, he collected his small trunk and other things and watched the other passengers who had gotten off. A woman said something about Loma Linda, so when a hack drove up and she got on, Oscar did also.

As he rode along, he remembered what he had heard about how the Seventh-day Adventist Church had acquired the Loma Linda property. The Adventists in California had built two medical facilities—Glendale Sanitarium and Paradise Valley—but they did not measure up to Ellen G. White's idea of a totally rural sanitarium. She had dreams of a place which would be a place not only for healing but for education as well. She concluded that it was neither Glendale nor Paradise Valley. Her dreams were so vivid, "I seemed to be living there myself," she said.

After a while she decided to investigate areas of Riverside and San Bernardino.

She wrote to an Adventist minister in Redlands named John A. Burden and told him to watch for property for sale at a reasonable price. In his search Burden found a site on an oval hill, called Loma Linda, Spanish for "Hill Beautiful." A group of physicians had acquired the property and had tried to develop a sanitarium here. They had already invested $150,-

000, but had continually lost money.

The institution's main building was a large frame structure containing sixty-four rooms. In addition, the property included four large cottages, a large recreation hall, and a pumping plant. Of the seventy-six acres of land encircling the sanitarium, eighteen consisted of orange and grapefruit groves.

Loma Linda was the place of Ellen White's dreams. It had operated for seven years when Oscar arrived. Only three years before, the institution had obtained a charter from the State of California, establishing the College of Medical Evangelists.

The cab let Oscar off at the Loma Linda Southern Pacific Railroad station. He went into the nearby sanitarium building and got acquainted with John Burden, the manager of the sanitarium. Then, fortunately, he met a Dane who had at one time worked at Skodsborg. Through him, he got a job as a gardener on the grounds, and his friend helped him find a room to stay in. He started his job as quickly as he could. And he began to take every opportunity he could to learn English.

CHAPTER

Oscar enlisted everyone's aid in learning the English language. Soon he had a whole circle of friends good-naturedly helping him. He studied with the nurses, he listened as hard as he could in church, and he bought an English Bible. Although he made a great deal of progress, it seemed slow to him.

To his deep disappointment, his sister did not come to Loma Linda, but remained in the East. Another sister and his brother Hartmann had come to America, also, and he was deeply grateful that Hartmann would escape the harrowing experiences *he* went through in the Danish army.

While he was working one day in one of the lush flower beds, trimming a rose vine, one of the other gardeners came up to him. "Hs-s-st!" the man whispered. "See that carriage coming?"

"Yah," Oscar answered.

"That's Sister White."

Oscar stared. "Why, this is the marvelous person who has had visions from God!" he thought. She had written *Den Store Strid* (*The Great Controversy*), which helped him so much in his suffering in the army, and *Aandelige Erfaringer,* which his uncle had said was *Early Writings,* the first book she ever wrote. His mother had loved that book, and his grandmother, too. And Uncle Ottosen was always consulting *I den Store Læges Fodspor* (*The Ministry of Healing*), for his work of healing became more meaningful by the counsel the remarkable woman received from God. While he stood there gazing, she turned and smiled. He wished he could speak English well enough to tell her how the words she wrote had been such a comfort in his prison cell in Denmark.

Working as a gardener even at Loma Linda was not the ladder which he wanted to use to climb to the high achievements he had set for himself. He learned of the Seventh-day Adventist college for Danes and Norwegians in Hutchinson, Minnesota, and decided it might be the place he should go. One night Oscar sat down and wrote to Elder M. L. Andreasen, its president, about attending the school. He also got in touch with Elder L. H. Christian, the president of the Lake Union Conference of Seventh-day Adventists, to obtain his help.

Oscar sold the books *Daniel and the Revelation* and *Steps to Christ* from door to door to earn money, and spent some time in Hutchinson. But he was still not satisfied. He found himself in the same situation there that he had been in in Iowa. Living among people who spoke Scandinavian languages, he wasn't learning English rapidly enough. At last he decided to do something his uncle had often urged him to do—take the nurses' course. Medical institutions desperately needed male nurses. Also he would give massages, and, in effect, be what we today call a physical therapist.

His indecision had taken him to Iowa, then to Loma Linda, and now to Hutchinson. It was about time he decided on just what he wanted to do with his life.

His brother Hartmann and his sisters had not wasted so much time. They were already at Melrose, Massachusetts, working on their nurses' training course at the New England Sanitarium.

He was jubilant when at long last his train stopped in Melrose. Hartmann and his sisters waited for him at the Boston and Maine Railroad station and took him out to the sanitarium. He got his room, unpacked his trunk, and prepared to stay.

Oscar Engen began the nurses' course in the New England Sanitarium at Melrose, Massachusetts, in the year 1915. He learned that the sanitarium used to be known as the Langwood Hotel. It consisted of a large hotel building with several other structures. They had their own electric lighting and steam heating system. The Adventists had purchased the group of buildings from a Dr. Coggswell, who had bought it planning to convert it into a hospital or a sanitarium. The sanitarium stood overlooking Spot Pond in the midst of Middlesex Fells, a natural woodland of some five thousand acres.

By the time Oscar became a student, the sanitarium had a new building, the original old hotel having undergone remodeling and repair for use as a residence for student nurses. It had also added hydrotherapy treatment quarters and a gymnasium.

At the New England Sanitarium Oscar faced a new problem. For a long time he had not had a chance to think about girls. While he studied and worked hard at anything and everything assigned him, he felt a growing loneliness for female companionship. However, rules about courting and men-women relationships were strict then around Adventist institutions. The administrators and staff watched the young men and young women closely. Oscar chafed under it. "How is a person going to find himself a wife?" he inquired of someone once. "You have to speak to people, at least, to find out if you'd like them."

"They're afraid it will—well, interfere with your lessons and your work," a friend said.

"But how is a person going to do his work well, with so many pretty girls in blue and white dresses flitting like butterflies, and a man has no chance to even get a *word* with a one of them?" Oscar persisted.

"Well, there are ways," came the cautious reply. "It's up to you to find them. Me, I've got a girl friend, and we're going to get married as soon as we graduate. But don't you tell on me."

"I won't," whispered Oscar. "But how do you do it?"

His friend shook his head. "No set way. I meet her in the hall, or a friend passes our notes. But we're careful. Don't want it known, see. So you keep still."

Oscar glanced over the student nurses, but not one of them appealed to him. Instead, his gaze kept turning to a graduate nurse and teacher, Bertha Umlandt.

As he thought about meeting her, however, he grew rather depressed. He was just a beginning student who could hardly speak English, while she was a supervisor. Besides, it was part of her duty to see to it that none of the women nurses slipped out to see the male nurses.

After Bertha had graduated in 1913, the sanitarium put her in charge of the women's hydrotherapy. She superintended the constant stream of patients who came through the gleaming cleanliness of the treatment rooms. She also taught first-year hydrotherapy and massage.

Oscar's sisters, Esther and Anna, were students under her.

One day they were working together in the hydrotherapy rooms. "Miss Umlandt, you must have had a lot of young men friends, with your curly hair and nice complexion!" Esther commented.

Immediately Bertha wrapped her cloak of dignity about her. "Nonsense!" she retorted. "I never had a boyfriend in my life."

"Ha!" laughed Esther, a trifle boldly. "You just wait. My big brother is used to fighting even *Lions*. He won't let anything like a few funny rules scare him."

The girls laughed as a warm apricot color suffused Bertha's pretty face.

But she regained her composure and smoothed her starched skirts. "Nonsense!" she said again. "I'm an old maid now and always will be." As she walked away, Oscar's sisters thought she appeared a little ruffled, but she seemed serene the next time they saw her.

When Oscar did start keeping company with Bertha, the faculty tried to protest. They warned and advised her, but Oscar did not let the opposition discourage him.

Time passed, and young romance began to work its magic. They started having little meetings in the rose garden, in the grape arbor, out on the lawn. But they did their work, and did it well, even though they were in love.

Oscar Engen graduated from the New England Sanitarium in September, 1918. That same month, September 18, Bertha Umlandt became the bride of Oscar Engen at the bride's home in Pennsylvania.

Life lay before the newly married couple. Seven years before, Oscar had expected to spend the rest of his life behind bars. Now he had the freedom of service in his beloved Seventh-day Adventist Church. With his bride beside him, Oscar Engen, son of the Vikings, prepared to face the future.

CHAPTER 17

After a sojourn in Wisconsin, where Oscar and Bertha lived for three years and where their oldest son, Hartmann, was born, and after a short term of service in North Carolina, the little family moved to Manchester Street in Battle Creek, Michigan, in the year 1923. Hartmann, Oscar's brother, already worked at Battle Creek Sanitarium in the men's hydrotherapy and bath department. Bertha and Oscar soon found positions also.

The sanitarium, a gigantic place, had a worldwide reputation for its diet, hydrotherapy treatments, and drugless healing. Conveyances met the trains at the Michigan Central and Grand Trunk Railroad stations to pick up patients who had arrived from all parts of the world. John Harvey Kellogg, widely known as a writer, surgeon, and inventor, headed the institution.

About one and a half blocks from the large Battle Creek Sanitarium stood one of the largest field stone buildings in the world, built by Neil S. Phelps, in association with his doctor brother, simply to put the Battle Creek Sanitarium out of business. They called it the Phelps Medical and Surgical Sanatorium. Dr. Kellogg had watched its construction with deep interest. Someone said he drove by one time, stopped, and watched the crew swarming over the rising structure. "Do a good job," he finally said to the workmen nearest him. "I may need it sometime."

Within four years, the ambitious institution went bankrupt, and eventually it became the Annex to the Battle Creek Sanitarium. In the months of July and August, the sanitarium's quarters would be filled to capacity—including the Annex—and the institution would have a long waiting list. The sanitarium had three large farms to supply fresh fruits, vegetables, eggs, and milk to the patients. At times it took over a thousand employees to operate the institution.

Oscar and his wife and small family moved into a modest two-story frame house about half a block from the Kellogg mansion. Manchester Street was the street of the elite. Lovely residences of doctors and staff members made it a genteel neighborhood.

Bertha's family now absorbed her energies. The children—Hartmann, Ruth, Otto, and Glenn—listened to Oscar tell of his encounters with important men in the sanitarium treatment rooms. J. C. Penney came to the institution, as did such men as Thomas A. Edison, Henry Ford, H. J. Heinz, Admiral Richard E. Byrd, John D. Rockefeller, C. W. Barron, of the *Wall Street Journal,* William Howard Taft, and Luther Burbank.

The children went to the church school and later to the Battle Creek Academy. Bertha nursed off and on through the years, never forgetting her skill in the healing profession. The extensive grounds of the Kellogg Estate were open to the children of that part of Battle Creek. Many a time Bertha took her sewing and went with her little ones, watching them while they played in the sand or paddled in the pool.

Oscar took care of men in nearly all walks of life, and with nearly every ailment known to mankind. Most of them he could nurse back to health, but with some he had to stand by their bedsides and watch them die. In many cases he helped them find Christ and a religious faith.

His experiences constantly reminded him that life and happiness do not depend on material possessions. One immensely wealthy patient confided one sleepless, pain-laden night, "Oh, Oscar, I worked all my life making money so that when I retired I would have a carefree and happy old age. But, now, I guess I worked too hard. I'd give all I have to get my good health back." He turned his face to the wall. "It's gone. It's gone forever. Oscar, I'm going to die!"

Another time Oscar was a special nurse for a famous industrialist who suffered a nervous breakdown. The sanitarium assigned Oscar to night duty with the patient. The man's illness particularly affected his memory. He did not remember what had happened to him as recently as a half hour before. At bedtime Oscar would give him a neutral, or relaxing, bath. But a short time later the man would say, "Oscar, it is time for my bath." Not wanting to argue the point with a patient who had been so ill, Engen repeated the bath. Soon he had to give the man three or four baths a night.

He tried lengthening the bath period and getting the patient to wait on himself as much as possible, to help him remember it. Oscar helped the man out of the tub one night and gave him a large warm towel, encouraging him to dry himself as best he could. Suddenly the patient stopped, looked at Oscar, and said, "Don't you think it just beats everything? Here I am paying a good price for my stay, and I'm hiring a day nurse and a night nurse besides. Now, why is it I have to do all this work myself?"

A happy highlight came to the Engen family and to the Battle Creek Sanitarium in 1930 with the visit of Dr. and Mrs. Carl Ottosen. It particularly delighted Oscar because of the tremendous impact Dr. Ottosen had had on his life. He shuddered to think of what might have happened in his life and career had it not been for his uncle's kindly interest in him.

Oscar was proud that his uncle had earned a reputation as one of the foremost physicians in Europe. In 1927, Dr. Ottosen had the honor of being knighted by King Christian X in recognition of the services he had rendered his country in the area of health and health education. The king was the son of the one who had pardoned Oscar.

Bertha had to run her household alone many times, for Oscar often received requests to go home with his patients and stay with them for a while during convalescence. One of Oscar's patients was the president of a large railroad. When he went to his home in a distant state, he insisted that his nurse accompany him. They rode in a private railroad Pullman car containing a kitchen, dining room, and sleeping quarters. Cooks and servants attended to their every want.

It was Oscar's custom, when he got a new patient, to have a talk with him and allow the person to unburden himself. One man, nervous and jittery, said, "Oscar, I've come here to get rid of my smoking habit. I'm afraid it's killing me."

"That is interesting," his nurse responded. "Other people may have come here for that purpose, but you're the first one to tell me that was the specific reason for your being here. What makes you want to get away from smoking?" Oscar asked him further.

"I've found out one thing," the other man said pointedly. "I'll have to lick this habit, or it is going to lick me. I'm a chain smoker. I can't even discuss business without lighting up one after another. I'm so nervous that I think sometimes I'm just going to go out of my mind."

"I'm glad, at least, that you are aware of what it is doing to you. Now, with your determination, I am sure we can win. But what about your wife? What does she think of this?"

"I'm sorry to tell you she smokes, too. But she says if I quit, she will."

"Good. We'll have a victory for two people when you quit."

"Should I quit at once, or do you think I ought to taper it off, and smoke a little less each day?" he inquired wistfully.

"Why don't you do this?" Oscar suggested. "Throw all your smoking materials into the wastebasket, and give me your pipe, as a souvenir."

The patient laughed. "I can do that," he said. "What else would you recommend?"

"Well," Oscar answered, "drink lots of water, more than you ever have in your life, to help you get rid of the poison in your body. Then—write your wife a letter tonight and tell her just what you have done."

The patient seized Oscar's arm, anguish and alarm in his eyes. "I can't! I can't!" he cried. "I have a terrible feeling that I won't be able to quit!"

"But you must burn your bridges behind you! That is what you'll be doing when you write that letter."

His patient struggled a great deal to break the habit, made some progress, but still could not bring himself to the point of writing the letter. But ten days later he came downstairs smiling. "I wrote that letter last night, Oscar, and it's true—true! I've gained the victory!"

Oscar never saw a happier man.

One patient made Oscar his confidant in everything. One day he called him and said, "Oscar, I have decided to end it all, for I am sure I can never get well, anyway."

Oscar knew that he had nothing organically wrong with him.

"The only thing that has prevented me from killing myself long before this is the thought of how hard my mother will take it," the young man continued. "You see, it's against our religion to commit suicide."

"I admire you," Oscar carefully answered, "for respecting your mother's feelings and for not wishing to go against your own religious beliefs. But it is against all good sense to do a thing like this. Let's not even discuss it."

It seemed to prey on the patient's mind, and he tried to bring up the subject again and again. But Oscar always tried to change the subject and to lead the conversation to more cheerful topics. He took his patient on long walks about the sanitarium grounds, always trying to convince him that he was really on the road to recovery.

One day the young man urged Oscar to let him go to town. "You see, I have a brother who is fond of hunting, and I'd like to give him a good gun for a present."

This aroused Oscar's suspicions, but he did not argue with him. "That's fine," Engen replied. "Let's go to town and select it. The devotion that you have for your mother and your brother is wonderful. I'll just go with you and help you pick it out."

The patient naturally seemed reluctant to have Oscar go with him, but he did not say anything. Oscar took him into several hardware stores, until he finally picked out a gun he wanted. After he pulled out his wallet to pay for it, Oscar told the clerk that the patient was buying the weapon for his brother and that the store should ship it to avoid trouble for the young man. The clerk said they would gladly do so and all he had to do was to give them the address.

Oscar's patient shoved his wallet back in his pocket. "I guess I won't take it, now," he said, turning away. Anger and disappointment showed on his face. He went with Oscar other places, but he didn't show much interest.

On the way back to the sanitarium, the patient bought a sports magazine. He read it for a while in his room, staring particularly at one page. Then he folded back a page and went into the bathroom.

While he was out of the room, Oscar went over to see what had so engrossed his patient, and found it to be only an ad for a patent medicine.

Returning, the man said, "I saw an ad for a wonderful medicine. I'm sending for it. It may help the terrible pains I've been having in my stomach." He actually ordered a revolver, advertised on another page.

A day or so later, he told his watchful nurse, "Oscar, my sister is sending me a box of chocolates. It ought to get here any day now." Again suspicious, Oscar kept his eyes open and said nothing.

For a few days they both watched the mail. Once Oscar commented, "I hope those chocolates will arrive soon, for I'm rather fond of candy. We will both have a feast."

Oscar's interest in his mail angered the young patient. But the staff of the sanitarium was on the job. Oscar got a call from the office one morning that the gun had come for his patient, and they had taken it to Dr. Stewart's office.

A few months of painstaking treatment cured the man of his suicidal tendencies. He went home, grateful for those who had taken an interest in him.

The years fled by, and Oscar continued his work at Battle Creek Sanitarium, doing his part to relieve a little of the world's physical suffering. The children grew up and went their various ways.

One of the grandest occasions in the life of Oscar and his Bertha came when their children held a golden wedding celebration for them in the parlor of the sanitarium. The oil painting of Dr. John Harvey Kellogg seemed to smile down on the occasion as if he knew a lot of things he could tell that would add to the honor. The children were there: Hartmann and his family from Virginia; Otto from California; Ruth from Loma Linda; and Glenn and his wife from Boulder, Colorado. Hosts of friends and loved ones moved about the decorated tables to honor two people who have been such a blessing to their world. It was fitting and appropriate that the celebration should take place in the sanitarium where they both had given so many years of service.

Some time later Oscar and Bertha—with Hartmann, Glenn, and Ruth—went back to

Denmark after his absence of more than fifty years. One day he stood in Amalienborg Square and saw the palace of the king and the changing of the royal guard. He realized that but for one-half inch in height, he might have spent his life in the army. He saw the old military academy where he last served his country after his pardon by the Danish king. And Skodsborg he found still a wonderful place of healing, a white village by the waters of the sea.

The dunes still drifted across Jutland as they had for ages, and the waters of his brook still flowed out to the cold waters of the North Sea, just as they did when Oscar paddled there as a little child. Archaeologists had dug up an old Viking ship from the shores where he used to play. But his father, with all his bluster and strength, and all of his neighbors had gone the way of mortal men. Only the old farmhouse and barns and outbuildings sat there brooding over the years that had budded and blossomed and gone.

Oscar Engen is a son of the Vikings. But instead of plundering and destroying as some of his ancestors did, he has spent his life building and healing. His forefathers may have sailed the seas, but when the pastor buried Oscar under the water at his baptism that June day in 1911, Oscar became a son of God. That is the greatest of all heritages.

We invite you to view the complete
selection of titles we publish at:
www.TEACHServices.com

We encourage you to write us
with your thoughts about this,
or any other book we publish at:
info@TEACHServices.com

TEACH Services' titles may be purchased in
bulk quantities for educational, fund-raising,
business, or promotional use.
bulksales@TEACHServices.com

Finally, if you are interested in seeing
your own book in print, please contact us at:
publishing@TEACHServices.com

We are happy to review your manuscript at no charge.

www.ingramcontent.com/pod-product-compliance
Lightning Source LLC
LaVergne TN
LVHW020640100826
845148LV00012B/2257

* 9 7 8 1 4 7 9 6 0 8 1 6 4 *